Praise for *The Holy Wild* [Grimoire]

"Danielle Dulsky continues to deliver the hard-won wisdom of ... overlooked or demonized archetypes in our bones. She so skillfully weaves the stories of the dead, the forgotten, the wild and unpolished, and the transformed into our own stories, so we may be transformed as well. Using the elements as a guide to illuminate our own rich histories and create rituals to honor them, *The Holy Wild Grimoire* encourages us to embody every magickal piece of ourselves. This is required reading for every Witch and heathen in this chaotic modern world."

— **Ora North**, author of *Mood Magick*
and *I Don't Want to Be an Empath Anymore*

"Are your words broken? Do they not land the same way they used to? Don't fix them, harbingers of your vanishing claims to mastery. Leave them where they lie on the floor, limp and expired, begging for hospice. Let your existential stutter, the inexpressible gasp for something different — for a different politics, for a sensuous animism, for a decolonial grammar — orient you through the wilds of this palimpsest. Limp through this irreverent handbook of spells, and it will conjure before you not more words but a glimpse of a world more alive than words could ever contain."

— **Bayo Akomolafe, PhD**, author of *These Wilds Beyond Our Fences:
Letters to My Daughter on Humanity's Search for Home*

"Danielle Dulsky's delicious writing never disappoints. A potent book of magick, *The Holy Wild Grimoire* is brimming with soul-stirring prompts and incantations that are sure to reignite your sparkle."

— **Trista Hendren**, creatrix of Girl God Books

Praise for *The Holy Wild* by Danielle Dulsky

"I sank into *The Holy Wild* like a seed into fertile, warm soil, and I was watered to my roots, shown how to flower, and sung into seeds flying free. Grab this book and savor it. It's a breathtaking achievement — thorough, practical, and straight from the heart and womb of the Mother."

— **Susun Weed**, Peace Elder, High Priestess of the Goddess,
and author of the Wise Woman Herbal series

the
Holy Wild
Grimoire

Also by Danielle Dulsky

The Holy Wild: A Heathen Bible for the Untamed Woman

Sacred Hags Oracle: Visionary Guidance for Dreamers, Witches, and Wild Hearts (with illustrations by Janine Houseman)

Seasons of Moon and Flame:
The Wild Dreamer's Epic Journey of Becoming

Woman Most Wild: Three Keys to Liberating the Witch Within

the *Holy Wild* *Grimoire*

A Heathen Handbook
of Magick, Spells, and Verses

Danielle Dulsky

Illustrations by Danielle Dulsky

New World Library
Novato, California

New World Library
14 Pamaron Way
Novato, California 94949

Illustrations by Danielle Dulsky
Text design by Tona Pearce Myers

Library of Congress Cataloging-in-Publication data is available.

First printing, September 2022
ISBN 978-1-60868-800-5
Ebook ISBN 978-1-60868-801-2
Printed in Canada on 100% postconsumer-waste recycled paper

New World Library is proud to be a Gold Certified Environmentally Responsible Publisher. Publisher certification awarded by Green Press Initiative.

10   9   8   7   6   5   4   3   2   1

To Maeve and her haunted lands

The Hag's Drum

I dreamt of a quake that rocked a lost land,
A shiver and shake in the sea and the sand.
My soul, it shook, too. My spirit, a moan.
I mourned like doves do then I called for the crone.

The healer who's seen such dark things before
The hag who's been to the Otherworld's shore
I'd find her and ask: What's a lost Witch to do?
What god or what task to devote this life to?

How might a heathen tend to this time?
When's the best season and what's the right crime?
I made a traveling cake and hummed a work tune
For my own soul's sake, I'd find that hag soon

I doused all my flames and stitched a red sack
I shed the old names when the thunder — it cracked!
The storm — it was here! — and I was too late
All I had feared would become my foul fate

I'd taken too long and still hadn't left home
My timing was wrong. I was far from that crone
Or was she here? The storm born from her drum?
Her rhythm was clear but from where did it come?

I wept for the answers I might never find
The poisons, the cancers, the cruel and unkind
I howled for them all, and the wind matched my mood
I was a ravenous squall and the old ways, my food

I dropped into that storm like a stone in a well
I surrendered my form to be shaped by this hell
I woke covered in earth, the sky wild with dawn
The air heavy with birth, the brutal storm gone

The elder had come, the world tender and new,
So I picked up my drum and danced like hags do.

CONTENTS

Love Letters on a Deathbed: An Introduction...1

Book One: THE BOOK OF EARTH
Heathen Verses from the Underworld 13

Word-Spell: Songs of Descent...14
To Begin Your Book of Earth: An Artful Invocation............................14
Story Lantern: The Homecoming of Deer-Woman............................16
Opening Spell: The Shape-Shifter of the Wild Earth........................21

EARTH REFLECTIONS..22
   Earth Reflection I: Hands in the Dirt.................................23
   Earth Reflection II: Permission to Descend.......................24
   Earth Reflection III: Memories of the Birth by Fire.............26
   Earth Reflection IV: Forbidden Fruit and Dark Wings
      Unfurled..28
   Earth Spell: A Gift for the Ground...................................29

EARTH PRESENCES..30
    Earth Presence I: Leaving the Polished Garden......................31
    Earth Presence II: Kissing the Serpent..................................33
    Earth Presence III: The Ritual Container...............................34
    Earth Presence IV: My Bone-Deep Tattoos..........................36
    Earth Spell: The Living Altar..37

EARTH VISIONS...39
    Earth Vision I: Underworld Rising..39
    Earth Vision II: My Wilder Home..40
    Earth Vision III: The Medicinal Brew....................................42
    Earth Vision IV: The Homecoming.......................................43
    Earth Spell: Marking the Moment..44

Testament to Earth..45
Possible Additions to Your Book of Earth...................................46

Book Two: THE BOOK OF WATER
Heathen Verses of the Sacred Rivers   47

Word-Spell: Songs of the Many Waters.....................................48
To Begin Your Book of Water: An Artful Invocation...................49
Story Lantern: The Queen of Holy Intoxication........................50
Opening Spell: Sipping from the Heathen Queen's Goblet..................60

WATER REFLECTIONS...60
    Water Reflection I: The Moving Prayer..................................61
    Water Reflection II: Secret Stories of the Holy Obscene.................62
    Water Reflection III: Saved by the Grandmothers.................63
    Water Reflection IV: Beginning Again...................................64
    Water Spell: Crossing the Threshold......................................65

WATER PRESENCES..66
    Water Presence I: An Unbridled Joy......................................67
    Water Presence II: The Quieter Side of This World...............68
    Water Presence III: Benediction to the Forked-Tongued
        Seductress...69
    Water Presence IV: Spells as Conversation............................70
    Water Spell: Wedding the River..72

WATER VISIONS...72
    Water Vision I: Art from the Fertile Dark............................73
    Water Vision II: The Liminal Space of Creation...................74
    Water Vision III: Witch of the Waves.................................76
    Water Vision IV: Water and Reclamation............................77
    Water Spell: Visions from the Well.................................... 78

Testament to Water..79
Possible Additions to Your Book of Water............................81

Book Three: THE BOOK OF FIRE
Heathen Verses of the Burning Temple   83

Word-Spell: Songs from the Pyre.......................................84
To Begin Your Book of Fire: An Artful Invocation...............85
Story Lantern: The Ire of the Fallen Mother.......................86
Opening Spell: The Oracular Fires......................................91

FIRE REFLECTIONS...92
    Fire Reflection I: The Ancestral Fire.................................92
    Fire Reflection II: Reclaiming the Flames..........................93
    Fire Reflection III: You Are the Crucible...........................95
    Fire Reflection IV: The Earth Bride..................................97
    Fire Spell: A Heathen Desire..98

FIRE PRESENCES..101
    Fire Presence I: Vows of the Fire-Keeper..........................101
    Fire Presence II: The Rage That Liberates.........................102
    Fire Presence III: The Original Oracle..............................103
    Fire Presence IV: What Lies Beneath................................105
    Fire Spell: Protecting the Hearth....................................106

FIRE VISIONS...107
    Fire Vision I: The Flames of Transformation....................108
    Fire Vision II: To Rise from Ashes...................................109
    Fire Vision III: The Weight of the Healer's Hands..............110
    Fire Vision IV: Hearth of the Heart.................................112
    Fire Spell: The Spiral of Self..114

Testament to Fire...116
Possible Additions to Your Book of Fire.............................118

Book Four: THE BOOK OF AIR
Heathen Verses of the Griever's Breath 119

Word-Spell: Songs of Breath and the Wild Hunt.................................120
To Begin Your Book of Air: An Artful Invocation...............................122
Story Lantern: The Blood Cloak..122
Opening Spell: A Storm of Infinite Potential......................................126

AIR REFLECTIONS...126
    Air Reflection I: To Die and Begin Again....................................127
    Air Reflection II: The Healer's Road..128
    Air Reflection III: The Ancient Antidote.....................................130
    Air Reflection IV: Becoming the Wolf-Woman...........................131
    Air Spell: Portals of the Haunted Heart.......................................132

AIR PRESENCES..133
    Air Presence I: The Breath of the Sacred.....................................134
    Air Presence II: An Elder Earth..136
    Air Presence III: The Circle's Soul...137
    Air Presence IV: Dear Innocent..138
    Air Spell: Love Thyself...140

AIR VISIONS...141
    Air Vision I: The Alchemy of Relationship..................................141
    Air Vision II: Like Honey Wine from the Magdalene's
        Tongue..143
    Air Vision III: The Ministry of Unanswerable Questions............144
    Air Vision IV: A Joyous Death..145
    Air Spell: Drumming the Heart..147

Testament to Air...147
Possible Additions to Your Book of Air...149

Book Five: THE BOOK OF ETHER
Heathen Verses from the Unseen Others 151

Word-Spell: Songs of the Cauldron Keeper...152
To Begin Your Book of Ether: An Artful Invocation............................152
Story Lantern: Return of the Mist Dwellers...153
Opening Spell: The Misty Bridge...154

ETHER REFLECTIONS...155
    Ether Reflection I: The Space Between..................................155
    Ether Reflection II: The Greatest Challenge........................157
    Ether Reflection III: The Witch's Psychic Soil.....................159
    Ether Reflection IV: The End of the Hunt............................160
    Ether Spell: Removing the Seer's Obstacles.........................162

ETHER PRESENCES...163
    Ether Presence I: To Live on the Fringes.............................163
    Ether Presence II: Sovereign within the Collective.............165
    Ether Presence III: The Language We Do Not Yet Speak.....167
    Ether Presence IV: To Be a Witch..169
    Ether Spell: Naming the Patterns.......................................170

ETHER VISIONS..171
    Ether Vision I: A Subtle Wink...171
    Ether Vision II: The Ancestral Story....................................173
    Ether Vision III: Washing the Dust.....................................174
    Ether Vision IV: The Spirit Wakes Wild...............................175
    Ether Spell: Asking the Dream-Weaver................................176

Testament to Ether...177
Possible Additions to Your Book of Ether...................................179
Holy Wild Spell: Gifting the Grimoire.......................................179

Conclusion...181
Acknowledgments...185
Notes..187
About the Author...191

LOVE LETTERS
ON A DEATHBED

An Introduction

Our heathen stories are the truest tales we know. Only in those se-cret memories where our feeling flesh meets the mystical do we learn our real names. Only in our own tales of death and resurrection do we understand the deep and mythic meanings inherent in our life story. To be heathen means to live on untamed ground, to peel back the dried, scaly, ill-fitting crust of who we were told to be, to claw our way up from the underworld and emerge with pomegranate juice gushing from our tongues and an incendiary desire to be known — to be wholly known — burning beneath our creaturely, mud-caked skin. Sometimes, these are the only stories worth telling.

In our more initiatory moments, we have a million names for death but only one for birth. This strange moment in the human story has called us all to name what truly matters in our world and retract our claws from the rest, from all that devours our resources but does not feed both our wild soul and the beyond-human world in return. Long-standing systems are being invited to die, their flaws of inequity and environmental negligence made more glaringly clear in the wake of the pandemic and mounting natural disasters. We can name so many forms of death now, but the births are still in shadow.

We ask ourselves if a good death for the most predatory ways of the world is possible, and we ask who we will become. If we chose to be here for this moment, what role will we play? Will we dance on the graves of ravenous capitalism and colonization? Will we be the mystic living in solitude or the open-armed healer who walks the streets? We can imagine a future full of space adventure and shiny metal conveniences just as easily as we can imagine a direr future full of floodwaters and fire. We can imagine the very wealthy enjoying the former future while the global majority contends with the latter. The seers, the Witches, and those many holy ones without a title understand that if we can imagine these futures, they are, on some plane, on some timeline, already real.

Even so, we continue to dream. We continue to imagine all possibilities, from a simple, slow life lived close to the land to one full of artificial intelligence and instantaneous movement. We can see it all, and we hold the tension between hope and despair. In our depths, we can still hear the pulse beat of the Holy Wild, and we know we are here for a reason. We know we are here to fulfill some strange and unnameable role, and we stand now in the dark, primordial void where all possibilities and all futures exist. In part, for now, we are here to ask the unanswerable questions:

What bones remain beneath the ash of the old, burned-to-dust dreams?
How do we better embrace generative confusion?
What does it mean to grieve well?
What if the remedy for apathy is awe?
How do we best befriend our uncivilized nature?
How can we explain experiences that transcend our language?
What if the future is far stranger than even we, the freaks, could ever imagine?

The Holy Wild is the unburnable essence, the primordial chaos of infinite potential taking form and dissolving, pulsing into and out of material existence. A forest burns, a land floods, but the Holy Wild remains. A star supernovas into an extraordinary and explosive demise, but the Holy Wild lives on, even in the unwitnessable darkness and silence that follow.

Our bodies are an ephemeral flesh-and-blood home for this primal material. The sacred sees the sacred through our eyes, and we are a living, heathen memory quilt of limitless incarnations. We were here, we are here, and we will be here; for this reason, our stories matter. Despite the many woundings we have endured, the betrayals and the rejections that left us weeping, our core essence remains.

The Earth is a cemetery for dead stars, after all. We all rose from a stellar boneyard. To be heathen is to remember why we were born into a feeling, creaturely body. We were born to sip the nectars of sweet joy and bitter grief. We were born to be living poetry, and we were born to behold a story far longer and larger than our own.

We chose to be here for these times, in this incarnation. We chose to be here to leave love letters on deathbeds and write eulogies for those old, orphaned dreams. We are a single line in an enduring ancestral story, and we cannot succumb to apathy any more than our grandmothers could. These are the days of the bone-people, those who shed the soft tissues of must-haves and should-bes and return to the most truthful center, the undiluted essence of what it means to be alive in a creaturely body in a time of intense metamorphosis.

Myths for the Moment

In times of unfathomable uncertainty, it serves us to find guiding myths, story lenses to look through and grant us a thankful foothold as the haunted underground rivers rise. Many of us orphans of modernity were not given our necessary mythologies, our maps for meeting the world, when we were younger. Many of us were instead given parables of original sin and forbidden fruit, of fallen women and resurrected men. Joseph Campbell writes that "it's a good thing to hang on to the myth that was put in when you were a child, because it is there whether you want it there or not. What you have to do is translate this myth into its eloquence, not just into the literacy. You have to learn to hear its song." The medicine arises not from trying to surgically remove these stories from our psyches, as if such a thing were even possible; it comes from letting these stories breathe, from breaking them out of the fire-and-brimstone-bordered prison they were sentenced to die in.

This moment in the human story wants a myth. This moment in our own smaller stories also wants a mythic interpretation, a peculiar analysis that offers a once-and-future connection between our own personal transformation and the global evolution of these times. Who are we in a postpandemic world in the midst of intense climate shifts? What old stories still have a thing or two to teach us about rebellion and belonging even now, even as so much of the outmoded order cracks and crumbles all around us? How might we make ourselves ready for what comes when we are wanderers who have lost our maps?

This world has seen such things before. If a story written thousands of years ago can teach us anything, it is that a place, a people, or a person can die and be reborn over and over again. An epic love story can start and end a war, cities can rise and fall, names might be shed and reborn, prophets can be executed and resurrected — and, through it all, the Holy Wild remains.

The New Old Story

The Holy Wild: A Heathen Bible for the Untamed Woman offers revisionings of the stories of women from the Christian Bible, women who have been historically framed as sinful, fallen, immoral, and heathen. *The Holy Wild* looks at these women through the lens of the five elements, discussing rituals and practices for liberating their stories and, by extension, the readers' stories.

If we look back on our lived-out-loud journeys, we find we have all been Eve tempted by the serpent and devouring the forbidden fruit. We have been a wild child stripping our skin of too-tight veils. We have been the prophetic mother, the weeping lover, and the defiant queen. Our own story is woven from the mythic threads of these well-known stories. To see ourselves in the faces of these women, repent nothing, and let the stories teach us something new is a radical act. We might ask ourselves: Who are we now that so much of our world has changed? If the etymology of *apocalypse* is a verb meaning "to lift the veil," who are we now that the veil has begun to lift, and who will we be once the veil has disappeared?

We could say all these women lived through an apocalypse of sorts. Their old world fell to bones. They were cast out, demonized, and killed.

They were each the shunned and shamed temptress. Even so, their stories hold lessons far beyond the historical subjugation of the feminine, far beyond the crumbling binaries of moral or immoral, pure or sullied. What do their stories have to teach us about this new and wild moment?

If to be heathen means to live on untamed ground, to dwell on the unbuilt fringes, to live a little closer to the Holy Wild essence of what we are made of, then it serves us to peel back the skin of the forbidden fruit from time to time, to ask why it was forbidden in the first place, and to see how our own experiences have reframed what *forbidden* even means.

To be heathen does not mean to exist in a vacuum where fierce individualism is king. On the contrary, to be heathen means to live so close to the Holy Wild that there is no separation between the human and the beyond-human. There is no divide between *human* and *nature*, and to speak of the natural world as something outside ourselves, something we need to reconnect to, is to reaffirm and fortify that separation.

To be heathen is to be cocreated by the elements, the weather, and the wild unseen, to have the long-vision and see beyond the boundaries we have been sold. To be heathen is not to reconnect with nature; it is to embrace and embody the understanding that our severance from the beyond-human is and has always been a lie. To be heathen is to heed the call to let our life be a microcosm of the collective we wish to seed in the coming decades, whether or not we are alive in this incarnation to see that collective bloom to fruition. To be heathen means to hold grief in the left hand and gratitude in the right, to adapt well and often, and to hone our night vision in dark times.

How to Work with This Handbook

By its most simplistic definition, a grimoire is a book of magick, a compilation of spells, ceremonies, and incantations used for casting, conjuring, and summoning the unseen forces. The etymology of *grimoire* stems from the French for "grammar," a humble origin for a word that now carries heavy weight in the occult community. In the context of this handbook, a grimoire reflects the magick locked in our language, the spells that live and breathe in our words and symbols. If all magick is communication, a book of magick shows the shell of a dialogue, the conversation starters and the etiquette, but it cannot possibly show the depth of the exchange. Every conversation is uniquely shaped by those who are speaking, by the choices they make and the worlds they live in, and this grimoire will be written for and by you.

In this handbook, there are verses, prompts, stories, and spells for deepening your encounter with the Holy Wild, with your own fundamental essence as it has been formed and re-formed through your unique story and shaped by this transformational moment in the world story. While *The Holy Wild: A Heathen Bible for the Untamed Woman* focused on reflection, on seeing the interconnectivity between your remembered story and the revisioned tales of the Priestess of the Wild Earth, the Maiden of the Unbridled Sensual, the Prophetess of the Wildfire, the Witch of Sacred Love, and the Queen of the Ethereal Divine, this handbook invites you to braid the past, present, and future, to curiously explore how these five elemental stories remain lusciously alive within you, give shape to your dream visions for a wilder future, and serve as a timely muse when story and awe are twin antidotes to the terrible poison of isolation.

You are invited to move through this grimoire at your own pace, in your own time. Each element has its own "book," and each book includes thirteen journaling experiences, in addition to spells and stories born of that element's medicine. You might set the intention to move through one entry each day, week, or moon cycle. You might binge-write an entire book — all thirteen entries — in one sitting. Follow your own road.

Each of the five books begins by offering a "word-spell," a "story lantern," and an "artful invocation" you will use to feel into that element's energy, to touch the medicine of the earth, water, fire, air, and ether. The story lanterns are often sharp stories, as they are born of myth; hold yourself tenderly while you read these tales of fallen mothers and intoxicated queens.*

The journaling sections in each of the five books begin with a verse from *The Holy Wild* — four each for *reflection* on the past, deep *presence* in the here and now, and wild *vision* for the future — but it is not

---

* All five of the "story lanterns" are inspired by Irish mythology. I write these stories from an Irish American perspective and acknowledge there is much I can never understand about these stories, as all the bones of my remembered dead are buried here on the Lenni-Lenape lands outside of Philadelphia, Pennsylvania.

necessary to read or reference *The Holy Wild* while you work with this book. The journal work is shaped by "word-witchery," a practice of using one's own writing as a form of spellcraft for manifestation, healing, banishing, and, most often, divination. The thirteenth and final journaling experience in each book integrates all three aspects of time — the past, present, and yet-to-be — inviting you to write your own personal "testament" to each element, to each face of the Holy Wild.

In these swiftly changing times, the only languages that make sense are songs, stories, and symbols. We require new words, and we must let the linear nature of our language evolve to be more liquid and less dense. We need to allow ourselves to be stranger than we have ever been, as individuals and as a collective, and we need to hand-build our own sanctuaries from love poetry written in tears and dedicated to the sacred places, to the myths that mark us, to the elders, to the children, to our people, and to our own aching humanity.

To that medicinal end, choose a sizable journal to accompany you on this journey through memory and muse. This blank book will become your personal grimoire, the house of your heathen testaments, and your soul-written bible that defines this moment you are living. Consider this to be a legacy book, a haunted memoir where all your ghosts will dance, a treasure you might leave tucked inside the hollow of a dead oak for a curious child to find, or a medicinal book of poetic light and shadow you might gift a lover just when they need it most. Here, may you write word-spells of paradox and wonder. May you make a starlit imaginarium of Earth reverence out of these ordinary pages. May you become a Witch of the word, and may you know your story as holy.

A Timely Invitation

The time to radically revision our place in the world is now. This is the moment in the human tale when hope meets sorrow, when innocence meets wisdom, a climactic union of polarities that is birthing — and will continue to birth — a new, more heathen reality. Reflect now: What about your changing world feels strangely and simultaneously possible and impossible? What has become less civilized — that is, less bound by industrialized norms, less limited by the confines of a religious system, less trapped by the reasonable and rational, or less tethered to the dominant culture's interpretation of what it means to be "good" or "bad" — during recent years?

Whatever your answer, look to these tender places where *this* meets *that* as teacher. Look to where apparent opposites are meeting one another in your perception and melting into each other in a bizarre, unprecedented fusion. These are places where your consciousness is undergoing a timely expansion, and here's the rub: this expansion is never finished. A star lives because the fusion continues, and dies when it stops.

We must continue to let ourselves be dazzled by our own befuddlement. We must embrace the eternal journey of falling apart and coming together, and we begin by looking at those soft places where old beliefs come to die. These are the fractures in the old foundations giving space for the wildflowers to grow. These are the places we might call forbidden, and it is there we build our new altars for a new time.

Between Rage and Awe: A Personal Note

Rage and love are not opposites. Every activist dances between the two. Consider what news stories make you spit vitriol and curl your fingers into fists. Can you see how this rage is born of a threat to, or betrayal or violation of, something or someone you love deeply? Love often undergirds a rage most righteous, and if we hold the tension between that rage and love, we sometimes see that the third brew that arises is awe.

I was born with an Aquarian sun and an Aries moon, with a brightly lit optimism and a vicious, sometimes singular desire to destroy obstacles that impede change. Hope is my fatal flaw. I began writing *The Holy Wild* in the summer of 2016, and I wrote primarily from a place of red-hot feminine rage and a love for women's stories, for women's resilience, and for Goddess. I wrote from inside the crucible, and I named ritual the remedy for apathy, as it had been my medicine in my more desperate moments.

I am writing this handbook now from a place of conscious awe. I have befriended a knowing in recent years that the world I hope to see bloom will emerge, in part because pieces of this withering world I love, as a white Irish American woman, are composted. I no longer name the Earth exclusively female; it is far too easy to frame all that nurtures despite systematic subjugation as *woman*. I can rage at the way women are treated in our society and understand that any identity that exists on the fringes of what the overculture deems acceptable will be subject to institutionalized oppressions. I can identify as a woman, see myself reflected back in the curves of a sycamore or the cycles of the moon, and understand that people of all gender identities see themselves there, too.

Breaking the Binary

The most potent medicine we have for these times is the vision of the *third road*, the invisible way we can see only when we radically refuse to frame the world in terms of opposites and dualities. There is no this or that; there is only *all*. As our old binary thinking begins to give way to something new, something we have not yet seen, the old systems that rely on opposition will rage and rebel against the heathen visionaries who can see beyond what has been. We will see good become bad and bad become good. We will see the left become the right and masculine become feminine. Our words will fall short, and no one will do this well.

We are heavy-bodied creatures. We are slow to evolve and quick to assume we know best; and yet, we are intensely, extraordinarily creative. The human animal is an artist by nature, and its imagination is infinite. When we begin to see the binary as limiting and seek to transcend it, dare to create new words and dream new futures, there are few boundaries to what we might become.

Love Letters on a Deathbed

This planet is not dying; to assume so is to center the human, and the dominance of the human is what has led us here, to the brink of climate collapse. Whether or not the human animal will survive the crises it has created remains to be seen, but Earth will most certainly go on. We are being invited now to fall in deep, all-consuming love with our world, to be seduced by the wilds, to allow the relationship that has existed between the humanity we might call *modern* and the planet to die so another can be reborn.

Any long-term relationship that survives does so because it has died many, many times. Every welcome rebirth in a relationship comes with a new way of communicating, a more genuine empathy, and a more mature intimacy. Salient questions for these times are: *How do we best midwife the death of the overculture's old relationship to the planet, and how do we kindle a new romance with this wild world that bore us? Can we leave a few love letters on the deathbed of our old and outmoded union, where the planet was a pretty thing to be pillaged by privilege, and write new vows for a new time?*

A Witch understands that their magick is cocreated by forces beyond naming, and there is an irrefutable magick to this moment for which we have no name. We must look to the bones of what we know to be true and let all else rot and fall away. We must slow down and let the world have its way with us over and over again, to tenderize our conceptions of what it means to be human.

In moving through this handbook, hold the tensions of the many memories, present-moment epiphanies, and visions that arise. Become both poet and prophet. Remember when the amber glow of a sunrise serenaded you at just the right time, and write a love song to that one wild morning in return. Be present to the ways your breath moves in waves like the rhythm of the sea, and envision a moment in the yet-to-come when you are swaddled in the deepest love by moonlight and mountains. Such exquisite beauty there is in these times. Such profound belonging might we find in a new relationship with this Earth we call home if we allow ourselves to feel, to really feel, how we *are* this planet. We are the sunrise and the seas. We are what we love about this world.

This is your tale of kinship with the Holy Wild, a love letter left on the deathbed of the old and a promise to let a few flowers sneak up through the cracking foundations of reason, linearity, and duality. This is a grimoire written by you for the in-between times, a nonanswer to the question of what comes next, and a bridge, built from eco-lust, between what was and what will be. To live in conscious awe does not mean to ignore the death counts or to spiritually bypass the work that must be done; we can write our grimoires and still march in the streets. To live in conscious awe means to be continually reminded of why we are here for this, and why we would not miss it.

Hold yourself tenderly now. You were born for these times. You are here because these patterns are yours to break. The poisons are yours to remedy. The new language is yours to speak, and the story is yours to tell. May we stitch a new flag from our tattered histories and wild aches, stand on the bridge between what was and what will be, raise our arms, and sing.

Book One

The Book of
EARTH

Heathen Verses from the Underworld

*I*n myth, the underworld is the realm of soul and shadow, death and initiation. In the Celtic tradition, the underworld is the place of the sea, secrets, and the ancestors. Far below our more sunlit landscapes, we recover missing fragments of who we are, puzzle pieces of our life story we have shunned and forgotten. In the reclamation, the old self dies, but the birth does not immediately follow. The death is essential for the birth to occur, yes, but the true initiation happens in the void between death and birth.

If we look to the mythologies of Sumerian Inanna, Oya in the Yoruba tradition, Greek Persephone-Kore, the Irish Morrígan, and other Goddesses of the Underworld across cultures, we see that descent is cyclical. We also see that the descent is not followed immediately by an ascent. The liminal time between the death and the birth is a period of composting and grief, a necessary gestation that has no schedule.

As you write your Book of Earth, allow time to move differently. Allow the many dissolutions you have experienced to be teachers, and permit a new poetry to emerge from their lessons. If the words do not come easily, draw images. Speak in symbols. Find solace in the in-between, the place where the true initiations occur. Nest yourself in the Great Below, in the subterranean caverns where the bones of the old selves still rest.

Word-Spell: Songs of Descent

Have you seen her lately? She's perched on a grave with a healthy dusting of dirt in her hair, spitting pomegranate seeds at her ghosts and singing songs of descent. They say she speaks the language of the underworld and only those who have been to hell can understand her stories.

Should we visit her, that mad vixen? She can see in the dark since she's come back, they say. She dreams in color but wears a tattered cloak of mourning. She repents nothing, not even her many nights spent with her ear to the Great Below, but she grieves well for the days she only danced around the forbidden fruit tree, daring not to even tread on its hallowed roots, biding her hunger for freedom's nectar.

I'm going to visit her now, I think. I'm going to sit beside her on that cold grave. I'm going to learn her new name and sing with her until she remembers the merit of those more innocent days. Then we'll sip that boneyard brew together and speak not only of our descent or our rising; together, this Underworld Goddess and I shall share the whole of our stories. We'll discount nothing. We'll sing the tales of our folly and our victory, of the obscene and the sacred. Together, she and I will be living memorial statues — humming, flesh-and-blood odes to the rawest myth, to the wilds of this eternal journey.

We speak the same language, you see. Her songs are my songs. Her story is my story, and the Holy Wild has birthed us both.

To Begin Your Book of Earth: An Artful Invocation

In the journal you have chosen to follow you on this journey, begin by drawing an image that speaks of a deep reverence for the earth element. Allow your memory to be muse and consider a fleeting moment in time when you felt seduced by a forest, a mountain, or the mud. Hold the tension of this embodied feeling while your hand moves across the page.

Do not overthink it. Let the lines be luscious in their simplicity. Leave your judgments out of the process and behold the beauty of this, your ink-and-paper ode to an earthen memory that marked you. Begin here, with your inner maker meeting your inner mage.

Allow each of the following questions to then spark another image, symbol, or word. Feel no need to answer these questions with rational explanations. Fill your page with this odd collage of nonanswers. Speak as the poet speaks. Sense the spirit already emerging from your Book of Earth.

What does it mean to be a human creature alive in these times?
How does the word *wildness* feel in your body?
When did you last descend into your underworld, risking rejection in the name of recovering a piece of your wholeness?
How did the Earth hold you in this moment of descent?
How does the Earth hold you now?
How are you a child of this planet?

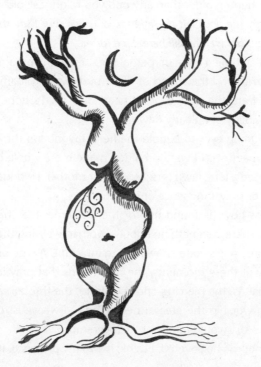

Story Lantern: The Homecoming of Deer-Woman

Read this story spell aloud if you feel called. Let it be a guiding lantern illuminating precisely what you need to know now, today, as you read these words. Add any images the story sparks or words from the story that feel potent to your artful invocation that begins your Book of Earth.

Some say the gods left these lands long ago, but I say the land is god. I, Deer-Woman, say we are still here. Sing for me.

Fools say I was cursed by a beauty that made me a target, but I ask you, what wild thing has not felt hunted by the long-fanged shadows? What creature lives on this Earth without beauty? I was pristine in my wildness. I was unbroken by life, and our story begins here, in the time of my innocence.

Can you see me, nested by the soft-running waters on an autumn evening, weaving sun wheels from dead ivy? Can you sense my peace? Can you hear my song? I come from a long line of shape-shifters, I do.

I am Deer-Woman. I am forest dweller, and I am more ancient than any human hunter, older than any god you might call old.

Some say the gods left these lands long ago, but I say the land is god. I, Deer-Woman, say we are still here. Sing for me.

I am deep time. I am a perpetual bud before the bloom. I am the eternal sun shower and the sound of night birds waking. I am what wildness dreams of. I am the slow-beating heart of a child's hope, and I am the infinite possibility of an early dawn.

Were human eyes to behold me here, I wonder if they would see me as you see me, just as I was, a maiden made more whole by her solitude, or if they'd see a lone fawn forsaken by her mother. I wonder if they would see beauty or prey, innocence or invitation.

This was how he found me for the first time, the Shadow Man, the dark mage. There is something about a woman weaving that speaks to our power, I think. A wise one knows not to interrupt. A wise one understands the sanctity of these moments, the holy hands that pray in deft dips and upturned palms, the piercing and the lifting, the through and the out. To weave is to worship the eternal becoming. To weave is to become god, and only a beast would interrupt such ceremony.

It was not me he coveted, I think; it was my presence. It was my peace he wanted to devour, my particular serenity he had never known. He wanted to make a sanctuary out of my flesh, to make me a refuge from his torment, and — I tell you this without a drop of that insidious poison called regret — I did not refuse him.

Some say the gods left these lands long ago, but I say the land is god. I, Deer-Woman, say we are still here. Sing for me.

His face was twisted in a pain I had no name for. He knelt beside me and bowed his head. He was shaking with a need I never knew, and in that moment, I welcomed him into the healing temple of my body. He wanted to swim in the waters of me, and I let him. He wanted to drink of the medicine between my thighs, and I let him. I was antidote to the baneful and bitter brew of his own forgetting, and there by the cool stream while the gloaming cast our bodies in a jewel-orange light, I helped him remember what he had lost, a bone-deep trust in his own worth as a wisdom keeper.

So, yes, I was the source of his rebirth. I was the reason he remembered the very magick he would use against me. I was his vessel of transmutation, his crucible, his fem-god. For years, he worshipped at the temple of me.

Some say the gods left these lands long ago, but I say the land is god. I, Deer-Woman, say we are still here. Sing for me.

I'll tell you now of something only the wisest ones understand: Sometimes, in order to reclaim even an ounce of forgotten self-worth, one must reject a god or two. Sometimes, a soul so weakened by the world seeks a certain vicarious power by kneeling at the feet of another they name holier than themselves, and, sometimes, that same soul has no choice but to spit on the very god they once named divine, if they are to truly heal.

It happens so slowly, this monstrous dance, but I could see it coming. I could see a flicker of disdain in his eyes when I told him I wanted to be alone. I sensed when he had to take a breath before speaking, as if he was straightening his mask. With every bit of his own power he regained, his disgust with me grew.

The Shadow Man, once so taken with the way I walked the Earth, whole unto myself, opening myself to others I deemed worthy, began to well with ire when he saw me with other lovers. His lips stopped dripping with love songs and started cracking under the heat of jealousy, and one night when all our people had gone to sleep, he bade me walk with him to the hazel wood.

Some say the gods left these lands long ago, but I say the land is god. I, Deer-Woman, say we are still here. Sing for me.

I believed this would be our final severance. I believed he was going to leave and never return, and for this reason only, I went with him. He had never harmed me before, you should know. He had never laid an uninvited hand on my skin, and he had never given me reason to believe he would use the most vicious magick against me, his healer, his lover, his friend, his Priestess.

The new moon was overhead this night, and I could hear the songs of my grandmothers echoing through the trees. I could feel them around me, and I knew it was time to harvest an ancestral treasure I had never before used outside my dreams; I had not needed to, but now I did. I had gone too far. We were too alone, and this was not the man I had known.

Fools say it was he who cast a spell on me, changing me into a deer as punishment for refusing his love, but this is not the way it happened. He would have killed me, that beast. He would have beaten me and left me there in the hazel wood to become food for the wolves, but my ancestors would not let that happen.

His cold hand gripped my arm, I wailed, and suddenly we were surrounded by a herd of antler-crowned creatures who spoke like I spoke, who dreamed what I dreamed. I could hear their words, and I took their direction. My snout grew long. My eyes grew sharp and wide. My limbs stretched longer and longer and longer still, because *no*, this man could not take my life from me. No, this man did not deserve my blood and my breath.

I house more magick in the pink of my tongue than he has in the whole of his bloodlines. He is a magician and a Shadow Man, but I am Deer-Woman joining the herd of grandmothers. I am mist keeper and green dweller. I am shape-shifter, and he cannot know the majesty that is me.

Some say the gods left these lands long ago, but I say the land is god. I, Deer-Woman, say we are still here. Sing for me.

Time moves differently in the creaturely realm, you know. I cannot say how many years went by, but I can tell you I was content in my wildness. The joy of wandering and loving and resting and belonging in this land is something many have forgotten, but the deer-people remember well. I spent those years learning the stories of my shape-shifting grandmothers, their names and their tales of birth and death. I learned wild poetry from the oak and the rowan, and I watched my human brethren from afar. I watched the Shadow Man become both feared and revered for his magickal skills. I heard him speak of how he enchanted me into a deer, doomed to be hunted for the rest of my short life. I heard him, and I pitied him.

There's no greater hex than pity, the wise ones say, but pity was all I had left for him.

My story might have ended here, but it didn't. It couldn't. In our travels, my sisterhood happened upon a band of hunters in their softest state, drinking and singing rebel songs at the fireside. One of the men had a way about him I could not name. He was human, but he had the eyes of a god. He was mortal, but everything he did was marked by the ethereal. He was ghostlike. He walked with one foot in each world. When he spoke and when he sang, it was as if the whole of the Otherworld was sounding a rhythm through him.

For hours, for the whole of the night, I watched him. I watched him sleep, and I met him in his dreams. I told him to find me when he woke, and I told him I would be the great love of his life.

Some say the gods left these lands long ago, but I say the land is god. I, Deer-Woman, say we are still here. Sing for me.

This man whom we shall call Finn woke to the sound of his hunting dogs barking with a ferocity he knew well, but when he found me, they were kneeling at my side under a yew tree. He was struck by the mythic in this moment, frozen by the sight of his vicious dogs whimpering at the hooves of a doe, and he dropped to his knees in a strange reverence. I let him see me then. I let him see my skin as the coarse hair dropped from my flesh. I let him see me as my spine straightened and my breasts swelled. I let him see me as no one had seen me in a very long time.

In love, we were. Some say the gods can't fall in love, but I'm here to tell you we can love so deeply a whole world might burn. I loved him. For a short time, I loved him.

One night, my Finn went out into the night to fight, and he left me, my belly full with child, safe in his stone house. I feared nothing in that place. My grandmothers had enchanted the lands with protection, and I was well guarded there.

Perhaps I had grown a bit soft in my human form. Perhaps I had forgotten the ways of the wild and the trickery of men, but I shall never forget the way he looked limping toward the house and calling my name. His voice sounded so wrong, so terrible, like every bone in his beautiful body had been broken.

"*Sadhbh! Sadhbh!*" I had never heard my Finn sound like this, and I ran to him. I left the safety of my place, and I ran to him. I ran to him like Macha racing the king. I ran to him cradling my fat womb, and by the time I saw his true face, it was too late.

Some say the Shadow Man returned for me, struck me with a hazel wand, and turned me back into a deer. The knowing ones understand he was there to strike me down forever, having heard of my happiness. Night after night, that Shadow Man writhed with an anguish over his unrequited devotion, and night after night, he had planned this moment.

That night did not go as it did in his vengeful fantasies, and in that moment, my grandmothers returned for me. My limbs and snout grew long, and I was Deer-Woman once more. We trampled the magician once and for all and, if I'm being honest, part of me died with him in that moment. When the Shadow Man took his last blood-soaked breath, I lost my will to remain human. I lost my desire for mortality.

Some say the gods left these lands long ago, but I say the land is god. I, Deer-Woman, say we are still here. Sing for me.

My child was born a shape-shifter like me. Many springs came and went, and little Oisin learned the language of the trees and became the greatest poet who has ever walked these lands. His father never stopped searching for us, and I stood in the shadows and watched when my babe finally met his father, my only human love. Finn knew his son's eyes, and he asked about me.

Oisin knew not to speak of me or the Others in our family, but he let his father see him shape-shift into a human boy.

"You are a wild child," my Finn said to him, and our little Oisin laughed. "Your mother will not come home, will she?" Finn asked.

Oisin turned and looked right in my eyes then. I shook my head, he shook his, and then he said, "My mother is home."

Finn must have known I was there. I think of this often now. He must have known I was there in the shadows, but he did not look for me. He did not try to pull me from my untamed world. He knew I did not want to be found, and this is the mark of a man, I think. He didn't try to lure me away from what I loved. He let it be my choice, and I made it. I made the choice to stay in the wilds, and he took little Oisin to live with him in the stone house, to bring his otherworldly poetry and tales of land spirits to the people.

I miss him, of course. I miss both of them. I miss the smell of little Oisin's fur, and I miss his stories. I miss the feeling of Finn's hands on me and the way he made me laugh. I miss them, but I would miss the forest more.

Some say the gods left these lands long ago, but I say the land is god. I, Deer-Woman, say we are still here. Sing for me.

Guiding Story Remembrances

Feel free to answer any or all of these queries in symbols rather than words, finishing your artful invocation that begins your Book of Earth.

1. What stage of the Deer-Woman's journey do you find yourself in now, at this point in your life?
2. What parts of the story, if any, feel like timely lessons for you now?
3. When have you been shape-shifter, moving into a form that lives closer to what you love?
4. What feels like your truest form in those fleeting moments when you feel the strongest kinship with the Earth?
5. What else did this story lantern illuminate for you?

Opening Spell: The Shape-Shifter of the Wild Earth

As you begin your Book of Earth, consider the landscape of your life now. See this mythic landscape with all your senses. What is the nature of this ground? From what direction does the wind blow, and what creatures walk this hallowed land?

Create sacred space by imagining yourself here, on this Earth, turning to the north and calling out to the shape-shifters of your lineage to come closer to you, to resource you in this moment. Turn east, south, and west, imagining your psychic lands as you call in the medicines of the four directions, of above and below. Speak spontaneous prayers to all directions throughout all times. Be Witch and bewitch. Pronounce your circle closed.

Breathe now, and ask yourself what new intention — what new relationship, gift, miracle, or way of being in the world — you would like to call in. Be as specific as you can. Slowly, surely, begin to see this new thing here on your psychic ground. As this new, strange imagining begins to take form, rock your body gently from side to side and chant: *Yes, I see. This shall be.*

As this new force is born — perhaps in the form of a creature, a star, a trail, or some other natural being or marker — know that something in your landscape may need to go. What feels as if it is dissolving as this change occurs? Remember that the wilds exist in perfect balance. If something new is coming, something old is leaving.

Keep chanting, noticing what you see. When you feel ready, if you feel ready, begin now to take the form of the new. Whatever transformation your landscape was undergoing to yield your desire, begin to embody this transformation. What are you becoming as you take on the energy of your desire? Move, slither, and shake accordingly. Come into a form that lives closer to your desire. Howl and sing. Become the embodiment of what you are calling in. Stay with this until you sense a shift in the space around you, as if the circle you have cast is somehow becoming fuller, more alive.

When you sense this change, offer gratitude out loud to this imagined world, to this dreamscape you have envisioned into being; this gratitude might come in the form of a hum, a song, or a dance, but let it come. Let these peculiar prayers of gratitude bring you back to your human form.

Open the circle when you feel ready, beginning with the west, then south, east, and north. To all the elements, to all directions, and to those unseen Others who bore witness to you in this moment, say thank you.

Notice the shifts that come from this small spell of shape-shifting as you continue your Book of Earth. Log the omens and synchronicities. Track your dreams. Stay vigilant.

Earth Reflections

The Earth is our greatest teacher. For all the knowing elders, wise innocents, skilled mages, and intuitive high Priestesses who have shared their stories with us, it is the land that holds the deepest lessons. These first four journaling experiences invite you to reflect on your relationship to the Earth as teacher, on the lands upon which your most pivotal moments took place, and on the places that gave ground to your many initiations.

The etymology of *reflection* is the Latin *reflectere*, "to bend back," and we are called to know any reflection as a mirror to who we are in this moment as the *reflector*. These reflections are not immutable. Our memory changes as we change. Our story is constantly being reordered, re-membered by and through us. Know that you may reflect differently on the same memory on any given day, and this is as it should be. Memory, like myth, is alive. I invite you to *bend back* now, to frame memory as oracle and see what reflections arise from these provocations. Through re-membering, we find that it is possible to change the past, and it is through this revolutionary act that our healing becomes radical.

Earth Reflection I: Hands in the Dirt

*"There is a part of you, my love, that remembers not only
your own hands in the dirt during childhood but the knowing
hands of your grandmothers and their grandmothers as they planted
their own seeds and connected to their own lands. There is a part
of you that is in a relationship with the earth element that most
certainly mirrors an intimacy shared with someone else in your
bloodline; the kinship she felt with the ground, the wounds of
her roots, the way she kept her home, her underworld fears,
and the shape of her body are all very like yours."*

Even in these time-impoverished days of brightly glowing screens, we live closer to the Earth than we think we do. Begin this first reflection, this first entry in your Holy Wild Grimoire, by asking an unanswerable question about belonging, the lands on which you have lived, or the lands of your people. This is a question that feels pressing but whose answer is uncertain. When you hold the tension of this question, there is a certain ache in the body, a tender sort of tension. Having read the above passage from *The Holy Wild*, what question arises within you?

In your journal, write and complete the following:

*I have an unanswerable question alive in my body now, and it's
    this:*

Letting your question be, without trying to find an answer, name your "teaching lands" and their greatest lessons. These are places of great importance to your story. These might be lands on which you lived for many years, places you visited only briefly, or places you somehow remember yet have never been to. You have many, but for now, list nine teaching lands in your Book of Earth. Feel free to grant mythic titles to these places, such as *Temple of Broken Slate* or *Forest of the Fallen Angels*; then begin to envision the spirits of these places as if they are entities.

What do the spirits of these places look like, and what did they teach you? What role did these teaching lands play in your story, for surely they were not merely passive backdrops to your wounds and healing, your griefs and joys?

For each of the nine teaching lands, use the following prompts or create your own, adding to your Book of Earth:

This land was my teacher, and it was named…
The spirit of this place has a wild look about it, with eyes like…
The lesson this land held for me was…

Looking back through your writing, do you notice any words that repeat? If so, underline these. Are there any potent phrases that stand out from your own writing that seem to be precisely the medicine you need right now? Underline these telling words, also; then look back now on your unanswerable question.

Have the words and phrases you underlined somehow given you an answer to your initial question? Reorder these words and phrases now intuitively. Become word-witch. See what wisdom emerges from your own words, concluding this entry in your Book of Earth as follows:

I asked [your unanswerable question]
The land teachers answered [your underlined words]

Earth Reflection II: Permission to Descend

"In our personal epic stories of wounding and healing, wandering and homecoming, confinement and escape, there is always a pivotal moment when a choice that seems to determine our destiny is made. In tales that reflect aspects of the Priestess of the Wild Earth

archetype, that choice is often to flee, to break free from the ties that bind the body and soul to someone else's expectations and seek out a truer, wilder home."

Choices are signposts that mark the crossroads in our stories. We might wonder who we would have become had we gone the other way, had we gotten on that plane, told that friend what we really thought, or gone home with that lover. Reflection on choices made is rarely an easy task, for our choices shape who we have become. When we consider the many crossroads along our journey, we are considering how easily we might have become someone different, someone who may hate what we love or claim a name we refuse.

The more distant from our choices we become, the more it seems our choices were not choices at all but rather the stuff of fate; in part, this is because of the immense discomfort we would find in considering that, yes, these were choices, and we easily could have gone north instead of south, left instead of right. So easily could we have become someone new. So easily can happenstance become destiny.

Name this practice as liberatory instead of confining. Name yourself shape-shifter and know you are cocreated by a number of forces, seen and unseen, that have uniquely weathered the current landscape of your life. Reflect on a single choice you have made within the last ten years, and grant that choice a mythic name, such as the *Battle of the Stone House* or the *Quest to Become*. Remember that you are naming the choice itself, not the direction you chose. Name the crossroads; then ask an unanswerable question about that choice, writing this question in your journal, continuing your Book of Earth.

> *I have an unanswerable question alive in my body now, and it's this:*

Holding the tension of this question, now consider who you might be had you made a different choice. Permit this inquiry to feel like a stretching in your imagination. Get weird. Who is the most peculiar version of you that could have arrived at the end of another road? What would they desire and grieve for? What might their name be? Describe this alternative version of you now, using the prompts I offer or creating your own:

This stranger chose to...
Their name is not mine, but they call themselves...
Their morning begins with...
They spend their days knowing...
They rest in...
Their world is not my world, but part of me wonders...

Looking back through your writing, do you notice any words that repeat? If so, underline these. Are there any potent phrases that stand out from your own writing that seem to be precisely the medicine you need right now, today? Underline these, also. Look back now on your unanswerable question. Have the underlined words somehow given you an answer, however cryptic it may seem? Reorganize these words and phrases now as if you are solving a puzzle, as if the version of you who is living on an alternate timeline to this one has somehow found a way to communicate in this moment, using the language of peculiar poetry. In your journal, conclude this entry in your Book of Earth as follows:

I asked [your unanswerable question]
The stranger answered [your underlined words]

Earth Reflection III: Memories of the Birth by Fire

"This is me, and I have survived my birth by fire.
My hair is knotted, and my cheeks are stained with the tears
of lost innocence and bitter disdain. I am untying the knots that kept
me tethered to a life I did not want, to names I did not want
to be called, and to the notion that a woman is an unchanging,
steady touchstone for all who need her."

An initiation, like a ceremony, comprises three key stages; this is true of our intentional ritualistic initiations as well as those rites of passage that seem to happen *to* us, that seem to usher us into a new way of being in the world that was both inevitable and not, it appears, consciously chosen. The stages of an initiation are the severance, the void, and the renewal. Importantly, none of these stages feel pleasant. No part of a true initiation is marked by comfort, and for this reason, it is normal to try to refuse the invitation for a time.

While it is difficult to perceive the stages of an initiation while they are occurring, we can reflect on our initiations and see the cyclical nature of the "birth by fire" chapters within our story. We are irrevocably changed by such alchemy. We are tempered and refined in the crucible of our own becoming, severed from our old roles and ways of being in the world, only to writhe in the primordial womb where the necessary gestation occurs, where time no longer moves linearly and the whispers of our ghosts are the loudest. Only after these stages of severance and void do we enter the renewal.

In considering your most potent initiations, afford particular attention to the void phase between the death and rebirth. There was a sense something had ended but the new beginning had yet to manifest. There was a definable death but no visible birth. So often, we reject this void phase, not considering it part of the initiation. There is an unsettling lack of certainty here. There is no closure. This is the grief space, and for this reason, the void is the most critical phase of initiation.

In this moment, ask an unanswerable question about this interim stage of initiation. You may have a sense you are there in the dark womb now, or you may need to reflect on a previous initiation. Know that an initiation is a process that changes you in an irrevocable way; you do not fully recognize who you were before. It can take years, or it can be over in a few hours. Whatever initiation feels most alive for you in this moment of reflection, ask your unanswerable question about the void stage, about that liminal cocoon space where the greatest transmutations occur. Continue your Book of Earth with this question.

I have an unanswerable question alive in my body right now, and it's this:

Now consider the physical spaces you were held by during this void stage. This may feel like a strange consideration since space and time are linked and time does not move the same in the void as it does in the ordinary world. By extension, initiatory spaces feel malleable. Sense the ways in which you were contained during your initiation's void, and now build a more fantastical version of this space.

You may have found that your surroundings — like the garden gone sour in the Priestess of the Wild Earth story from *The Holy Wild*, where the trees suddenly appear plastic and the landscape too carved and pruned to be wild — seemed to be changing because *you* were changing, when in fact the space had stayed relatively static. While in the void, what was your perception of your space? You may use the prompts I offer here or create your own:

I don't know how it happened, but suddenly the world seemed...
The temperature shifted, and I felt...
*There was a timely alchemy to this place, and the walls dripped
    with...*
The ground teemed with...
The sky was not a sky but a...
All the while, I could hear the voices of...

Looking back through your writing, underline the words that repeat. Underline the potent phrases, the words you don't remember writing, and any strange prophecies that stand out to you. Revisit your unanswerable question about the void, and reorder your words and phrases to form an answer, however prophetic and bizarre. Imagine yourself gifting this answer, this medicine, to the version of you who is cocooned in that void, who is swaddled in darkness and still breathing, against all odds. Conclude this entry in your Book of Earth as follows:

I asked [your unanswerable question]
The void answered [your underlined words]

Earth Reflection IV: Forbidden Fruit and Dark Wings Unfurled

*"Every time the gritty marrow of the fruit touched her tongue, she
caught a glimpse of her destiny. With every hearty swallow, she saw
the rainbow shades of her liberated life."*

To taste the forbidden fruit is to question what we have been told, to refuse to outrightly accept the rules we have been born to. To taste the forbidden fruit is to evolve beyond our more stringent disciplines, to admit that maybe, just maybe, there is a larger world outside the one in which we have been living. To admit such things takes immense courage, as it requires us to expand our vision beyond the center and toward the fringes of what is acceptable not only to others but to ourselves.

Consider your own experience with the forbidden fruit. Who told you it was forbidden, and why? How did the tasting of what was named *bad* expand your perception of not only the world but yourself? What poetry can you see in the movement from limitation to liberation? And last, is it possible that the forbidden nature of the fruit gave you a necessary container within which to grow? Ask an unanswerable question now about the forbidden fruit.

> *I have an unanswerable question alive in my body right now, and it's this:*

Reflect now on the moments leading up to the tasting of that forbidden fruit. Do you remember where you were, what sounds you were hearing, the scents in the air? Write of these memories in your Book of Earth now, using the prompts I offer or creating your own:

> *I am here, about to taste…*
> *The light is strange, and I wonder…*
> *There's a tension in my being that tells me…*
> *If I name this fruit as medicine, then what ails me is…*
> *Now I am…*
> *But after this forbidden brew touches my tongue, I will be…*

Breathe, return to the writing, and, as before, underline the words that repeat, the potent phrases, and anything that feels channeled. Look back at your unanswerable question and shape an answer from your writing. Imagine the forbidden fruit itself gifting you this wisdom, and conclude this entry in your Book of Earth.

> *I asked* [your unanswerable question]
> *The forbidden fruit answered* [your underlined words]

🪔 *Earth Spell: A Gift for the Ground* 🪔

This is a simple spell of finding great beauty in the forbidden, of offering a gift to the Earth. Hold an apple in both hands, and consider it a mythic image. Breathe deeply. Consider your dream visions for a world made more whole, for the children of the future, and for yourself. Begin to name these wishes as *must-bes*. Hold the tension of the desire. Sense your past and future ancestors surrounding you and speaking these present-tense prayers with you and for you.

Whisper the transformations you want to see in the healing beyond-human world, especially those shifts that still feel forbidden, that would upset the more damaging power imbalances that have ravaged the planet. Let the fruit hold it all, every willful prayer and every hex of systems you would like to see fall. There is much wisdom in knowing what you do not desire, but be sure to also name what you *do* want to see the Earth become.

Feel these intentions low in the body. Plant them like seeds in your soul. If the words stop coming, sing. If the song stops coming, hum. Keep going. Say all you can. When you feel ready, hold the apple to your heart and whisper one last blessing. Dig deep. Get your hands in the dirt. If you are unable to plant the apple in a wild place, use a pot full of soil. Plant the apple, along with a gift for the ground such as spit or a strand of your hair. Press your hands into the ground after the burial and feel the tender poetry of this moment.

You are here, a child of the Earth. And so it is.

Earth Presences

To be present to the teachings of the earth element is to consciously participate in our own creaturely story. Here, we name nothing as fixed. Here, we are gifted the opportunity to behold the exquisite landscape of our lives in all its imperfect glory. We see so clearly what is dying and what is dawning, and in our more generous moments, we welcome the whole of life's dance.

True presence does not require joy or comfort. We can be present to our sorrow and our rage just as we can be present to our ecstasy or ease. True presence does ask us to break the cage of linear time around every cell in our body, to feel a closer kinship with our wilder ways. Linear time is a tyrannical ruler, and much of the overculture bows to its reign.

The lessons of the earth element are slow and deep. Once we absorb the lessons of the mud and the root, however, we do not easily shed these understandings; they take up residence in the bones, and this is how we know we cannot return to the way we once lived, to the places that once claimed us.

Earth Presence I: Leaving the Polished Garden

*"Rebellion against what is not ours precedes
the reclaiming of what is truly for us."*

In Jungian psychology, the archetype of the rebel is synonymous with the revolutionary and the destroyer. To rebel is not simply to reject and escape. To rebel is to act against, to deconstruct. The etymology of *rebel* is the Latin *re-* + *bellum*, "to renew the war," and coming home to the earth element is never a smooth journey unmarked by at least a bit of mayhem.

The particular kinship we have with the earth element lives in our roots and is intricately mirrored back to us through our relationships to home, food, money, belonging, and body. These are, of course, weighted categories that have been greatly distorted by capitalism, colonization, white-body supremacy, and other like poisons. For this reason, it is important to not uniformly equate your relationship to home, food, money, belonging, and the body with your relationship to the Earth.

If you are human, you are of the Earth, and you belong here. This exquisite planet of pleasure, pain, and all that lies between and beyond is your home, and all you require to live is here. It is the function of long-standing and oppressive power structures to enforce notions of scarcity, to continually tell us there is not enough for the needs of all to be met and met well, to create and empower institutions that ensure the disproportionate wealth and health of the privileged. Belonging is not a commodity to be bought and sold. To rebel against what is not ours means seeing what does not belong in our world as individuals but also what does not support equitable change for *all*.

Rebellion is the first act of discernment. Knowing what we don't want is just as important as knowing what we do want, though the latter is often much harder to name. Ask an unanswerable question about something you know in your roots, in your bones, you do not want in your life and in the world. This should not feel like a dead question arising from memory; this query should feel quite alive in your depths, right in this moment. Continue your Book of Earth by posing this question.

I have an unanswerable question alive in my body right now, and
     it's this:

Be present to this question and hold its tension. Of the aforemen-
tioned five categories related to the earth element — *home, food, money,*
belonging, and *body* — which seems most closely related to your question?

Allow your imagination to get stranger now and grant you an image
or a symbol of your question. This image or symbol might not make
sense. This is how your creaturely mind is choosing to show this question to you in this moment. See the peculiar image and draw it in your
journal as you see fit. If you feel called, find a place where this image or
symbol can safely and ethically sit and be held by the wild; perhaps you
paint it on a rock or draw it in the sand. When you feel ready, you may
write to continue this entry in your Book of Earth, beginning with these
prompts or creating your own:

The symbol spoke not in words but in ...
If I name this shape my teacher, it might just show me ...
In my bones, I know that home is ...
In my roots, I feel that food is ...
My gut tells me money is ...
One thing I know for sure is I belong to ...
My body is comforted when ...
I do not want ...
I want ...
I do not want ...
I want ...
I am forever rebelling against ...

Underline the words that repeat here and the sharp phrases that
seem to hold much meaning. Look back on your unanswerable question and shape an answer from your writing, concluding this entry with
the following:

I asked [your unanswerable question]
My inner rebel answered [your underlined words]

Earth Presence II: Kissing the Serpent

"May you be willing to exist on the fringes in the name of liberation,
finding and belonging to those wild circles of openhearted seekers
who make you feel as though you are a larger version of yourself
and leaving those circles where entry always demands you wear
a too-tight mask to disguise your true face."

Relationships must be allowed to breathe, to wax and to wane in a balanced cycle of becoming. So often, our circles become like the Priestess of the Wild Earth's garden, suddenly too small and ill fitting. This does not mean we need to condemn those relationships as toxic or surgically remove them from our stories. We must remember that sometimes our circles have remained the same while *we* have changed. Our friendships, our partnerships, and our teaching circles may not have transformed at all, but we have; for this reason, the circles no longer serve us, but this does not mean they never served us.

Consider the circles to which you belong now. These can be small or large networks of people related to any life area, including but not limited to work, spirituality, creativity, family, play, or learning. Choose one circle on which to focus for this practice, and ask yourself in what ways you show up most authentically here. Ask a question now about this particular circle and your role in it, beginning this entry in your Book of Earth with this question.

> *I have an unanswerable question alive in my body right now, and*
> *it's this:*

Repeat this question aloud in the heart voice, a whisper. What conditions do you seem to require in order to show up without a mask in this particular circle? Can you name your particular needs from this circle? Are they being met regularly? What do you feel you bring to this circle? What particular gifts do you offer to these people, and are there boundaries set around this giving and receiving? Does the relationship feel balanced, like breathing? When you feel ready, you may complete these prompts or create your own:

The circle once was…
The circle has become…
The circle will be…
To them, I offer…
To them, I can no longer offer…
From them, I require…
From them, I no longer require…
I'm in love with this circle's…
My deeper desire is to…

Look at your writing and underline the words that repeat here, along with any information that feels new or potent. Return to your unanswerable question and shape an answer from your writing.

I asked [your unanswerable question]
The circle answered [your underlined words]

Earth Presence III: The Ritual Container

"Here, in ritual, we set boundaries around our life transitions and make the mundane magickal."

A ritual not only embodies a clear intention; it houses a whole epic story from its ordinary exposition to its extraordinary lysis. A ritual marks you. Done with intention, a ritual can change your world, gift you with clearer sight, grant you a new name, and provide a space in which the rivers of time flow in strange circular patterns. For all these reasons, a ritual requires a strong container.

Be present to a particular transition you are moving through currently. You might choose a small transition or one that feels life altering. You might choose a transition that feels nearly complete or one that is just beginning. Once you have decided on the particular life area you will be working with, feel into the story of this transformation and how you might wish to be held by ritual as you experience this metamorphosis. Pose a question now about this transition.

*I have an unanswerable question alive in my body right now, and
it's this:*

Now, look at your question without trying to answer it. How might
a small and solitary ritual be remedy for this uncertainty? Importantly,
the ritual may not answer your question for you but will be the medicine for any discomfort you may feel around the not knowing. The ritual will not only name your uncertainty as valid; it will be cocreated by
the unknown and unseen. Continue this entry in your Book of Earth by
considering this ritual and the following questions:

Can you name a sacred place that could provide the container
for this ritual?
I've named this place the holy ground of...
How will you acknowledge sacred space once you are there?
*This place was sacred long before I arrived, but today it
shall become...*
What small offering can you make to the land in gratitude for
being your ritual ground?
To this place, I offer...
When you arrive, what words will you speak that will mark the
ritual's beginning?
"I've come here to..."
What words will you say only with your body?
I am becoming...
What words will you speak aloud at ritual's end, knowing that
plans go only so far in ritual?
"I'm leaving with a knowing, a knowing that..."

When you feel ready, carry out this ritual, surrender to the unseen forces that hold you, and be witnessed by the loving ghosts who
know you best. After you have completed your ritual, revisit your unanswerable question. Underline words and potent phrases from your
ritual-planning writing and/or any additional reflections on the ritual
experience itself. Conclude this entry as follows:

I asked [your unanswerable question]
The ritual grounds answered [your underlined words]

Earth Presence IV: My Bone-Deep Tattoos

"Recall the wisdom of your grandmothers and all who came before you. From whatever Earth-based traditions your lineage hails, whether you know of your ancestral history or not, envision your roots tapping into a dark well of primordial feminine knowledge, swirling and bubbling and holding the very medicine you need right now. Soak the wisdom up through your roots."

If we move back through deep time far enough, we see that we all come from a tradition that lived in rhythm with the natural world, that revered the cosmos and named nature god. Such knowing has been locked in the marrow, housed in the bones and blood, until the time was right and the world was ripe for a reclamation of what we have always known to be true: We are a creaturely folk. We are meant to live slower and closer to the land, and our biology has not caught up with the pace of our techno-driven society. Ask an unanswerable question about lineage or land, beginning this entry in your Book of Earth.

> *I have an unanswerable question alive in my body right now, and it's this:*

Breathe deeply and imagine you house a wealth of secret medicines and cosmic maps inside your cells. Invite the ancestral field in this moment to gift you with a symbol of your unique, inherited knowing. Do not try to rationalize this symbol or understand what it means quite yet. Know this now only as your "bone-deep tattoo," and describe it in your journal when ready:

> *I've got a secret recipe stamped on my ribs, and it's for…*
> *I've got a brew in my blood, and it's called…*
> *The grandmothers gave me a remedy for every…*
> *In my bones, I know…*
> *Through their eyes, I see…*
> *If these secrets were a song, I would sing out for…*
> *Just for today, I am naming my gift…*

Look at your writing and underline the words that repeat here, along with any information that feels new or potent. Return to your unanswerable question and shape an answer from your writing, concluding this entry in your Book of Earth as follows:

> *I asked* [your unanswerable question]
> *My bone-deep tattoo answered* [your underlined words]

❧ *Earth Spell: The Living Altar* ❧

This is a ceremony of deep reverence for your ancestral story, for the many generations that have come before and will come after your bones are feeding the ground. Hold the long-vision now; you are a sovereign being here on this Earth at this time, yes, but you are a single word within an epic, multigenerational poem full of grief, gratitude, and grace. You may feel alone in this moment, yes, but you are surrounded by those long-gone-still-here ones who know you, who still breathe through you.

Go to a wild place if you are able, and ask permission to be there. If you sense you are welcome, begin by honoring this as hallowed ground. Take a moment to breathe and orient yourself. Befriend the directions. When you are ready, you will become a living altar of earthen presence.

Face the north and ask yourself where the wisdom of this direction lives in your body. Become a living gesture now to the north, holding yourself in such a shape that you are a breathing statue of reverence to this place. Imagine your ancestors and children of the future mirroring you, holding their own bodies in this same shape, speaking these words as you speak them: *To the north, to my loving ancestors and the yet-to-be-born, to the sacred energies of the soil and seeds, to the green dwellers and mountain ghosts, I say welcome. Bear witness to this, my ceremony of grief and gratitude.*

Feel the energies of the Earth rising from the ground and climbing your bones. What is the song of these energies? Let them sing through you now. Hold yourself here and sing. Sing for those old ones who came before, for you, for innocence, and for the sacred planet.

When you feel ready, turn to the east. Become a living statue for this new direction. The beloved dead mirror you as you speak these words: *To the east, to my loving ancestors and the yet-to-be-born, to the sacred energies of the smoke and wind, to those who bring the dawn and mark the morning with song, I say welcome. Bear witness to this, my ceremony of grief and gratitude.*

What new song arises now? Let it come. Channel the song of the wind, the chants of the trees. Whatever sound comes, know that it is perfect. This is the voice of the wild coming through you. Let the resonance take root in your guts. Become a living drum. Let it come. Let it come. Let it come.

Stay here for as long as you have; then turn to the south. Sense the heated wisdom of this direction, and shape yourself to honor this place. Hold yourself just so. You are a living statue to the rhythms of the south as you speak these words: *To the south, to my loving ancestors and yet-to-be-born, to the holy energies of the flames, to the fire tenders and altar builders, I say welcome. Bear witness to this, my ceremony of grief and gratitude.*

Let the song come now, arising from the molten core of the Earth. Feel the fire in your belly and sing a song of flame and ash. Sing for the serpents and the desert storms. Sing for hearth, heart, and home. Sing until it feels finished; then turn last to the west.

Sense the wisdom of the west. Where are the energies of the west in the body? Hold yourself in a way that honors these unnameable knowings. You are a living altar to the direction of mystery, shadow, and paradox. Feel the unseen Others coming closer, and speak these words: *To the west, to my loving ancestors and yet-to-be-born, to the sacred energies of the oceans and rivers, to the death Priestesses and the sea hags, I say welcome. Bear witness to this, my ceremony of grief and gratitude.*

Let the west sing through you now. Yours is a song of waves and wonder, salt and sea. Let the waters hum through you like river undercurrents. Hear the waters of your blood hum. Sing for those who have left this world well. Sing for those who died alone. Sing for those babies who are so bravely erupting into the world right now at this moment and for those who are taking their last breath as you sing, sing, and sing.

When it feels finished, come into one last gesture of grief and gratitude. Hold the tension between these two fertile states of being and spontaneously speak your own prayer, your own song, your own offering to the elements, seen and unseen.

And so it is.

Earth Visions

What might we see if the rhythms of our lives slowed to match the rhythms of the Earth? What once-and-future songs might we be gifted with if we dared to carve out long hours from our days for stillness? How in tune to the seasons of our lives might we become if we made a holy practice of bearing witness to the running streams and windswept fields?

We are surrounded by oracles in this wild world of ours. Every stone can be a teacher if we behold its beauty long enough. Every windblown blade of grass can be a pendulum, every mud puddle a scrying mirror. Every seer knows the merit of silence, stillness, and participation, and like a good story, our Earth Visions cannot be rushed.

Earth Vision I: Underworld Rising

*"The descent is necessary, for only from our depths
can we begin to rise."*

When we find ourselves in the underworld — confronting our shadows, shedding our masks, and relinquishing outmoded notions of who we are and where we belong — it is not the time to behold the larger story of our life. No one writes their memoir in the underworld. No one finds peace while they drown in the underground river of grief, abandonment, or betrayal. The rising takes time, and healing is a slow process of awareness and integration.

Consider one of your many descents now; this might be a time of illness, the loss of a loved one, or an unintentional initiation that might go by many names. Choose a scar, but do not choose a wound that still bleeds. Without reliving the descent, ask an unanswerable question about this time in your life and begin this entry in your Book of Earth with this question.

*I have an unanswerable question alive in my body right now, and
it's this:*

Now ask yourself whom you needed when you were lost in the dark. Who would have been your ideal underworld guide at that time when you were experiencing a death of your old world? Did you want someone to show you the way out? Did you want someone to simply sit with you in your depths, cook you a hot meal, and listen? What would your ideal healing elixir have been at this time? Let it be part fantasy, as many of us did not have such protectors when we needed them most. Describe your medicine keeper now, using the prompts I offer here or creating your own:

The medicine keeper had eyes of…
They told me to always remember to…
They gifted me with…
They sang me songs of…
I still remember their wisdom in my moments of…
So blessed were they to have been born with…
If I could see them again, I'd thank them for…

Go back through your writing and underline the words and phrases that stand out to you. In particular, underline the descriptors of the medicine keeper. Ask yourself now to what extent you embody those qualities. How are you *that*? We become the teachers we needed when we were younger. We become for others the medicine we needed, and there is such healing in this knowing. Craft an answer to your unanswerable question from your underlined words and phrases, concluding this entry in your Book of Earth as follows:

I asked [your unanswerable question]
The medicine keeper I have become answered [your underlined words]

Earth Vision II: My Wilder Home

"We tell ourselves we cannot have what we truly desire, for that very desire will get us kicked out of the life we know. We tell ourselves we cannot have what we want, particularly when that longing does not conform to the individualistic goals of our inner Fathers, those masculine commanders who rule over our psyches as if they were armies, fighting against anyone or anything we deem foreign or unfamiliar."

If nothing else, the lessons of the Earth teach us to befriend our own rhythms, our many cycles of becoming and unbecoming. We are in a constant process of learning and unlearning, and the heart of any spell, the well-defined intention, arises only from discernment. Only when we can clearly say *I want this* are we able to call it in, and such knowing demands we distinguish between what we want and what we have been told to want.

The Irish Goddess of sovereignty, Queen Maeve, demanded her lovers be able to name their desires in a single breath. She required their devotion as well as their discernment. Sense where the objective energy of desire is in your body. What color is it? What temperature is it? What shape? If you could ask a question of your own inner desire, what would it be? Begin this entry in your Book of Earth with that question.

> *I have an unanswerable question alive in my body now, and it's this:*

Witches have the long-vision. Witches understand that they are a lone breath in a long ancestral story. In your solitude, what is it you desire for this holy planet of ours? What do you hope will become of our blue-green cosmic parent, and what will need to be unlearned in order for your desire to come to pass? Consider these weighted questions, using the prompts I offer here or creating your own:

> *I have a vision of an Earth that has become home to...*
> *I want to tell the children's children's children that...*
> *The songs sung in this wild future are of...*
> *Somewhere, on some plane, this vision of mine already exists, and there I see...*
> *It's my secret, but I'm going to call this Earth the...*
> *Here, time means...*
> *Love means...*

Go back through the writing, underline the words that seem to mark you, and then stitch together an answer to your unanswerable question, concluding this entry in your nearly complete Book of Earth as follows:

> *I asked* [your unanswerable question]
> *The yet-to-come answered* [your underlined words]

Earth Vision III: The Medicinal Brew

"Now, bewitch this garden-hell from the inside out."

We stand on that tender edge between gratitude and grief when we consider our desires for future generations. We hold the tension between hope and sorrow, aching possibility and utter impossibility. Consider Earth in the 2900s, nine hundred years from now, and write an unanswerable question about this strange world, beginning this entry with that question.

> *I have an unanswerable question alive in my body now, and it's*
> *   this:*

Allow this question to spark a small understanding now, a dim flame burning in a room full of shadow, and ask yourself: *If I had nine months left to live, what would I do with my days?* You may use the prompts I offer here or create your own:

> *I decided to live the way I always knew I could live, with...*
> *I left behind...*
> *I moved toward...*
> *One day, I found myself...*

Underline the potent words and phrases, and now ask yourself what a typical day looks like for those living nine hundred years from now, in your dream vision for what the world might become. You may use the prompts I offer here or create your own:

> *They wake every morning knowing...*
> *They spend their days...*
> *By dusk, they breathe and understand...*
> *They go to sleep every night knowing...*

Consider now the extent to which your description of your final moons here on Earth aligns with your vision for the yet-to-come world. Underline the words and phrases that stand out to you from the dream-world writing. Draw from your underlined words and phrases for all prompts and craft an answer to your unanswerable question, concluding this entry in your Book of Earth.

> *I asked* [your unanswerable question]
> *The dream vision answered* [your underlined words]

Earth Vision IV: The Homecoming

"She saw herself handcrafting a new life out of her crystalline
passions and mud-brick talents; it was a life well worth the sacrifice
of loneliness, grief, and rage, and she would risk everything
and anything for such freedom."

Our memories are always parent to our inspiration. In times of generative befuddlement when the question "What do you want?" has no easy answer, we can look to our holiest moments to point us toward the next steps on our journey. Ask yourself to recall a fleeting moment in time when you felt so fiercely present, when your whole body and soul were in flow with the elements. You were there, and you were not there. You were cocreated by unseen forces. You felt witnessed somehow in this moment of pure, unbridled presence. Hold the tension of this memory and ask an unanswerable question about that ephemeral moment in time, beginning this entry in your Book of Earth.

> *I have an unanswerable question alive in my body now, and it's*
> *this:*

Permit your memories to be an oracle now, and try to name ten more moments like this, when a sunrise was your god or a laughing circle of friends was your ceremony. Name all eleven moments now in your journal, describing them just enough in your Book of Earth so that you know which memories you are referring to; then notice what patterns exist in these moments.

Are you often alone or with friends? Is it often a certain time of day? Are you immersed in nature and held by the elements? If so, which elements seem dominant in your named memories? Make a list of at least three patterns you can see in these moments; then imagine building a ritual out of these patterns. What would this ceremony of homecoming look like? You may describe it using the prompts I offer here or create your own:

> *This is my ritual of coming home to soul, and I am...*
> *There is a new secret name I am claiming, and it's this:*
> *I am grieving for...*
> *I am grateful for...*
> *On this, my holiest day, I am calling in...*

Underline the words and phrases that feel important, and consider carrying out this ceremony if you feel called. Use your underlined words and phrases to craft an answer to your unanswerable question, concluding this entry in your Book of Earth.

> *I asked* [your unanswerable question]
> *My ritual of homecoming answered* [your underlined words]

Earth Spell: Marking the Moment

This is a small, spontaneous spell for marking the moment, for making a memory out of the present. We all have moments when we suddenly feel met by a deep awe, a sudden, unexpected, and fleeting instant when the world shows us how holy this land really is. An eagle flies low overhead, and we find ourselves stunned into a sacred silence. Thunder rolls over the hills, and for a reason we cannot describe, our bodies become still and we have no choice but to listen.

The next time you find yourself in one of these moments when time stops, when you are suddenly younger than newborn and older than ancient, do not rush away too soon. Stay, breathe, sense the exquisite beauty in this lone crisscross of time and space where you find yourself somehow held by the elements. Make a memory out of this moment. Whisper words of gratitude. You are here, rooted in the land and blessed by the sky and sea. You are here, nested just so in this holy, wild world.

Testament to Earth

The first "testament" in your Heathen Testaments will be for the Earth. Allow this Testament to Earth to conclude your Book of Earth. Begin your testament by writing an invocation to the earth element. You may use the prompts I offer here or create your own:

> *This is my testament of mud, mountain, and stone, and I am*
> *   welcoming a wilder way to…*
> *I am asking unanswerable questions of…*
> *To the Earth, I say…*

Go back through your Earth Reflections, Presences, and Visions, and look to the last line from all twelve journal entries. Stitch these together to become your "Earth Verses":

> *Verse 1: The land teachers answered…*
> *Verse 2: The stranger answered…*
> *Verse 3: The void answered…*
> *Verse 4: The forbidden fruit answered…*
> *Verse 5: The inner rebel answered…*
> *Verse 6: The circle answered…*

Verse 7: The ritual grounds answered…
Verse 8: The bone-deep tattoo answered…
Verse 9: The medicine keeper answered…
Verse 10: The yet-to-come answered…
Verse 11: The dream vision answered…
Verse 12: The ritual of homecoming answered…

Complete the final prompt below. Then read your Earth Testament aloud in a sacred place, and if possible, follow the reading with a time of silence. Be witnessed by your ancestors. Be held by the land. And so it is.

I am here, held by the land, and I know…

Possible Additions to Your Book of Earth

- Write a brief, three-part memoir of initiation. Part I focuses on your ordinary world, who you were before some great death of the old self sent you deep in the caverns of shadow and darkness. Part II describes your time in the void; you were there, and you were not there. Your world was changing irrevocably, your old names had been shed, and you seemed to be outside time. Part III describes your ascent, your reentry into the light of day, and your healing.

- Create a "forbidden fruit" recipe where every ingredient represents a "right" that you feel ready to claim, though your people may not understand, though the powers that be may disapprove. Perhaps an apple represents your right to create fearlessly, brown sugar represents your right to sensory pleasure, and cinnamon represents your right to speak and be heard.

- Allow your Earth Testament to be muse and design your own solitary ritual of devotion to a particular place that feels sacred to you. Make note of which solar and lunar season would best house this ceremony, which ingredients and other materials you might need, what the intention is, and how you will acknowledge sacred space; and craft a loose description of your process. Leave room for the ritual to be cocreated by the land and those unseen Others who know you best. Be Witch and bewitch.

Book Two

The Book of
WATER

Heathen Verses of the Sacred Rivers

*B*efriending our feeling flesh is honoring our creaturely nature. The water element has much to teach us about expression, the senses, and the fluid nature of our emotions. We are creative animals. We all have an art we are born to channel. The pure essence of our particular genius is the rushing waters, and our wounds, joys, rages, desires, and griefs are the rocks that give shape to the flow. No two rivers share the same curves, depths, and currents; so, too, is there an art only you can create. There is a story only you can tell, and your scars have made this so.

To have *flow* in our lives does not mean to relinquish all resistance and boundaries. To flow means to have the right resistance and intentional boundaries for our creative essence to move through the world as we want it to. How can you shape the vessel in such a way that a fluid surrender within this container is possible, beautiful, and nourishing? How might the tales of your many wounds and wants be wielded, be placed just so, to carve just the right map for your artist's river to flow as it should?

These are the questions the water element teaches us to ask. Our water spells are those we cast in the name of creative expression, healing clarity, emotional integrity, and unapologetic sensuality. Our water stories are those that mirror the Goddesses of art, fertility, and sexuality. Look to the tales in your traditions where creation meets lust, those origin stories where the rivers of blood run thick. All creation myths show us that no birth comes without destruction. Our generative impulses to express something new, to make meaning from feeling, are not always sweet. Here, we may still wonder what will become of us, but we are grateful for having been born to this feeling flesh nonetheless.

Write your Book of Water from a spirit of flow, taking notice of when the words pour from you relentlessly and when the story feels dammed. Allow new waterways to be molded as you write, and be wary of following only the existing patterns, those deeper ditches dug long ago where the flow stagnates. Allow the writing to shake something loose with each entry in your Book of Water, and become that wildling dancing naked in the river, shedding the ties that still bind too tightly.

Word-Spell: Songs of the Many Waters

Running clear and clean in my dreamscape is a mighty river rushing over crystalline stones. In my more desperate moments, I hear the songs of these waters. I hum in time with the rhythm of this perpetual flow, and I bathe my too-hot thoughts in the open chill of ancient currents. I am lust in a liquid. I can feel the infinite wonder of this holy place, and even now when my ache is not so great, I can sip from this vision and come home to the abundant waters of my belonging.

Raging gray and wild in my dreamscape is a storm-tossed sea crashing against black crags. On my most ireful evenings when the world seems so broken, I hear the anthems of this deep and majestic well from which I was born. I sing. I howl the songs of the sea when the thunder rolls in from the west, and I am held by the pulsing poetry of this old salty grandmother spirit. Here, I am in awe of these times. I am a living ode to the kelp forest dancing beneath the torrent, and I am the mystic shadows of the unseen abyss.

Melting slow and swift in my dreamscape is a sovereign glacier poised to break and drift. Here, I am a dream most tender. I am a living ache weeping for the wilder-than-human world, and my tears are returning their salt to the rising waters in a grief ceremony for the winters that will never be. I am a banshee's eternal wail. I am in communion with the ghosts of the more frozen seas, and here, I am a creaturely body full of warm blood and am remembering a more conscious future into being, one foggy breath at a time.

Reflecting the amber dusk in my dreamscape is a still mountain lake encircled by queenly pines and ancient sycamores. Here, I see the fabric of time stretched long on this liquid mirror. I see the poetry written by the earliest evening stars, and I hear the songs of my ancestors humming from the underwater caves. I am here. I am of these waters, and these waters are of me. Here, I am miracle. Here, I am free.

To Begin Your Book of Water: An Artful Invocation

In the same journal you have been using for your Book of Earth, now begin your Book of Water by drawing an image that reflects your truest form of creative expression at the moment. This is a soul symbol, an image that howls forth the rawest parts of your story. Envision yourself in a watery place. Hear the sound of the waves or songs of the falling waters. Be here with all your senses and create a mythic image that speaks to this vision.

Allow each of the following questions to then spark another image, symbol, or word. Just as you did at the inception of your Book of Earth, fill your page with your strange responses to these queries. Honor this, the birth of the spirit of your Book of Water.

What does sensual freedom mean to you?

When do you feel safe to express yourself creatively? What conditions do you require?

What does your forbidden dance look like?

What fairy tale seems to reflect your journey of *coming home to self* most closely?

What is your secret name, the name you have never told anyone?

Story Lantern: The Queen of Holy Intoxication

Read this story spell aloud if you feel called. Let it be a guiding lantern illuminating precisely what you need to know now, today, as you read these words. Add any images the story sparks or words from the story that feel potent to your artful invocation that begins your Book of Water.

Some called me queen. Some called me a living, heathen appetite. Some called me a God-Witch and brought me offerings of honey and milk. Even so, no one knew my real name, not even when the painted-blue children danced atop my bones in loving memory of their holy, wild mother.

Some say the gods left these waters long ago, but I say the waters are god. I, Maeve, say we are still here. Sing for us.

Some called me the Drunk One. Some called me medicine woman. An ecstatic beast, I was, an ever-boiling-over pot of bitter wine. The inebriated monks who stole and twisted my myths were not my enemies but my unwitting dedicants, sipping from the royal goblet between a Pagan queen's legs night after night, falling into a wild sleep where they would be sucked dry of their purity, where those skin-starved men would meet the insatiable living intoxicant that was me. By day, they claimed a saintly new religion. By shadow, they were on their knees before a flame-haired vixen, begging to crawl 'neath her skirts once more. How else would they know my stories?

I had to possess them, you see. I had to mark them, and mark them I did.

To meet me, they would say, was to be initiated into the secret order of the sacred obscene, to know divine death, and to drink from the upturned drum of red and raw justice.

Some say the gods left these waters long ago, but I say the waters are god. I, Maeve, say we are still here. Sing for us.

They say three rivers of blood flowed forth from between my thighs and carved the land. They say, too, I was born from these rivers called seduction, appetite, and justice. I was the maker and the made, you see, the mother and the wild child. I was source and substance, and these waters witnessed my pain and my becoming, my rise and my fall. Now, these waters witness my resurrection.

Before you hear my tangled tale of time spun 'round on itself and how I, Maeve, became crowned the queen of sacred inebriation and holy lust, I must ask you to unlearn what you think you know about boundless drunkenness, battle, and heathen intoxication. I must ask you to tuck your rules and your warnings away in a treasure box and humor me.

What if you are whole and well and it is your world that is sick, and what if — my love, *what if* — all your feverish quests for wholeness required, in the end, not a submission to some distant and dominant god but a once-and-future belief that there was a land that longs for you as much as you long for it?

Perhaps you see a face now that is not your own, a face of some twisted lover with whiskey breath or a traumatized soldier with a drowned memory or a small-boned slurring sister or a lonely student or hunted Witch who lost themselves to the needle, the pill, or the drink. Perhaps you were all of these at one time, the abandoned child in a grown body, with wine-stained lips and fermented honey in your veins.

I might ask you now, as I stare into the rising currents from which I was born: "Is that you, Maeve?"

There is an acute horror called amnesia of the sacred, and the gods know it well. A recent affliction, this peculiar and prophesied impairment. A dying virus, they say. A dilution of the senses and a fog in the mind. A heavy mold has collected in the ears of our creaturely dedicants, and those fragile-skinned orphans can no longer hear us. Their eyes have been sunscorched by the brilliance of their many screens, and those poor wanderers are blind to the march of the ghosts and the raucous runs of the wild hunters all around them, even now, when their world is falling to bones at their feet. Even now, they cannot smell the fecund rot of death from which their new world will be born, for their noses have been tuned only to the sweet and savory. Even now, their tongues are numb to the taste of death, and their feeling flesh can scarcely glean the heat of my breath, yet I am still here.

Do not despair. There is something else the gods know well, and that is this: Those afflicted creatures are their own antidote to the poison of forgetting. They carry the remedy in their marrow, you see. Tucked away deep in their psyche, buried in the under-kept root cellar of dream visions and lost symbols, is a knower's map, a wayfinder, a mythic compass that would point them right here to this blood-born river if they were only to stop, to dig, to be radical in their resistance to reason.

"Is that you, Maeve? Do you hear me?"

Wash the dust from your ears and your eyes now. Anoint your nostrils and awaken your tongue. Touch your own lips and bid me come a little closer. Whisper aloud: "Is it me, Maeve?"

I am the transcendent awakening of chosen kings. I am the wine and the chalice, the water and the well.

"Is it me, Maeve?"

I am the blood Goddess of the green lands. I am the righteous battle and the fated death, the rotting corpse and the winged scavenger with guts dangling from my aged beak.

"Is it me, Maeve?"

I am the enchanted mare. I am the slow-boiled flesh and the divine feast, the grief and the celebration.

"Is it me, Maeve?"

I am unbridled presence. I am not an escape in the sloth of drunken debauchery. I am the considered consumption of a holy drink. I am not a sloppy weekend bender. I am the queenly humility of trusting the chosen intelligence of intoxication. There is nothing I am numb to. I feel all.

"Is it me, Maeve?"

You're goddamned right; it's me. I am the worm in the eye of the fallen white bull. I am the silent drum, the unlit match, and the empty cauldron. I am infinite potential embodied in a long-running ancient river where myths gush forth and knock into rock after rock, where the stories spill into the ancestral sea before they, again, feed these old rivers of memory.

Some say the gods left these waters long ago, but I say the waters are god. I, Maeve, say we are still here. Sing for us.

You know the wilder stories of me, mayhap. Have you heard I needed thirty men a day to satisfy me? It's true. Have you heard I tested all my lovers by forcing them to state all their desires in a single breath? It's true. Have you heard of my visit to the sun portal, my encounter with a fat-fleshed Fae-woman who gifted me my most sacred mead recipe? It's true. Have you heard I was killed by a piece of hard cheese or started a war to be equal to my husband? This is only part of the story. Have you heard of me as a hag-woman harbinger of death? A banshee with a bowl of blood?

"Is it me, Maeve, that hag?"

Have you heard I was buried upright, sword in hand?

"Is it me, Maeve, the bones in the ground ready to fight?"

Some say the gods left these waters long ago, but I say the waters are god. I say we are still here. Sing for me. Drink with me. Sing for me. Drink with me. Drum for me. Dance with me. Howl with me.

Are you ready?

This is the story I really want you to know. A timely tale, this. Sometimes, a sort of apocalypse lifts the veil between the creatures and the gods. Sometimes, though not often, a crack opens in the ground beneath a fortress those angry orphan kings thought impenetrable. Once every few hundred years, the amnesia of the sacred becomes so great, the loss of the land stories so desperate, the world has no choice but to begin a great and massive correction.

Sound familiar?

I hear you, you know. I hear the Witches screaming at midnight in the name of an impossibly possible world. I hear every beat of their heart-drums, and I hear their once-and-future songs.

I hear you when you scream into the dark: "Something must change now! We cannot go on like this!" I hear you, and I hear the land.

Sometimes, I come to the living Witches in their dreams. I intoxicate their reality and call them to action. Sometimes, they find just the right medicine they need in my myths.

A story can save a world, you know. A story can raise a religion and destroy a kingdom. So here's a story for you. When you hear it, draw no conclusions. Not yet. Let it take root in the fertile soil of your psyche. Water it with song, and see what becomes of you and this wild world you live in. See what you remember of kings, bad seeds, and redemption.

Once upon a time long gone that still is, there lived a king we might call... good. He revered the land that was me, and I saw him — do you hear me? — I saw him, this king, kneeling and whispering prayers to the hazel roots that he should rule well, that the land should speak through him, that he should remain humble even when so many bowed at his feet. What would it be like to have a ruler like this in your world? Someone who belonged to the land, a steward of the rivers and mountains who understood that justice was the work of repair and not punishment? What would it be like to trust a leader?

This king knew me, you see. This king lit candles in my name long after he'd been crowned. He didn't cast me aside after his initiation, as so many do. He remembered. He remembered that the land and the people thrive when the Goddess is content, and it was a sound partnership, his and mine.

This good king had a lone flaw, though, as they all do, and this king's particular flaw was impatience. The gods keep a different clock, you know, and when the king begged for a child, we heard him. I heard him. I was going to bless him with a babe that would be a ruler even more brilliant than he was. I was going to, but the king couldn't wait.

He summoned the Witch from the woods and begged her to give him a child. "Cast a spell on me and my queen, Witch. For all our nightly efforts, we are childless."

Now, I'm going to tell you a secret: this Witch from the woods was me.

Sometimes the gods grow bored, and we want to feel something. We want to be born, and we want to die. We want to feel the rain on our face, and we can do that only if we are born to human flesh, and I was in precisely such a way when the king was afflicted by his longing. A human lifetime is but a single breath to a god, so the choice to incarnate and feel something for a moment is much like your choice to eat a bit of chocolate or take a sip of tea, so I cannot really say anything more than that a Witch was a good person to be for a bit, and a Witch I was.

Of course, I was a little annoyed he hadn't simply waited for his prayers to be answered. I was irked by his impatience, so I decided that yes, yes, I would grant him a child, but I would test him first. I told him, this king, that he needed to take the queen into the oak grove on summer solstice and make love to her there just as the sun sets. I told him further that they should sleep there in that grove, and at sunrise they would wake to find there at the place of their coupling five acorns in a circle and a lone purple heather flower growing at the center.

The king started to protest that heather flowers never grow on their own, but I shushed him and continued, saying that the queen must eat the heather flower without touching the acorns, and if she does this, she will surely become pregnant with a wild and just child, a daughter who would rule as he ruled, with a sound mind and Earth reverence.

"Whatever you do, don't take the acorns from the grove. Don't let them even touch your hand," I said. A small ask, I thought.

Now, the king and queen did everything just as I asked, and they drifted to sleep satiated at midnight, sure in their love for one another and the promise of a soon-to-be-birthed babe. All seemed right and well that night, and no one — no one, not even I — saw this next part coming.

Sometimes a trickster enters the story, you see. The trickster is neither good nor bad. The trickster jumps in from the fringes, tosses things about, then leaves just as swiftly. The trickster in this story is one of the fair-folk, a spritely thing who had been watching the ritual from the shadows. At dawn, as the sun rose and the royal-violet heather flower sprouted between a circle of acorns, as the queen stirred and reached carefully for the flower, just when the king thought all would be well, the little trickster faerie swept in, snatched the flower, ate it, giggled, winked just once, and left.

Now, the king and queen were beside themselves. They both knew full well there would be no finding the Fae. They could wait until the following year, they supposed, until next solstice — but, again, the king was very impatient, and his impatience clouded his judgment in this moment.

Against my advice, the king gathered up all five acorns and put them in his pocket. Surely some of the same magick would be in these acorns, would it not? Surely these holy oak seeds would have some of the spell in them. The queen protested, they say. The queen understood that a Witch's warning was something to be heeded, but the king was arrogant in his wanting. That day, the king soaked the acorns in water and fed them to the queen, not knowing what he had just done.

There was a rattle in the kingdoms of sky and sea that day, and the gods knew that something terrible had taken root inside the womb of the queen. Her belly swelled quickly, and in just three months' time, precisely at the autumn equinox, she gave birth to five sons. Just as the fifth babe erupted from between her thighs, she took her last breath, and the king was left alone with five terrible monsters who shared his blood.

The gods say that the five sons of the good king were born at the beginning of the Great Forgetting, seeds of destruction, you might say. Each of them had a particular addiction born of a tragic god-loss. They never really knew me, you see. Born of folly and impatience, they were. Born not to a fool but to someone who had a foolish moment.

The oldest among them was called Greed, and you might say that he was the worst among the brothers. Even as a child, Greed could never acquire and hoard enough of whatever it was he loved at the moment. He needed to have it all, and when he had it all, he needed more. Such insatiable hunger does not exist in nature, do you know? Even the most voracious predator does not consume until it bursts, yet Greed did.

You might wonder how such a good king could raise such a son, and this is a reasonable question. Some say he just wasn't paying attention, and some say he himself was beginning to be lured by the sweet reward of conquest. Some say he was simply without a woman and was quite busy with his other four sons. An unsavory lot, they were.

His second son was called Distance, and like Greed, Distance was afflicted with a disease of the modern. Distance could never go far enough away from home. He was always traveling; not a bad thing, you might think, but he was so concerned with getting away from his place that he never really befriended this land he was born to. He took me for granted, you see. He dreamed of building great ships and sailing to other worlds that might become his. He dreamed of planting his flag on mountaintops and building great walls. His ways were those not of the nomad but of the colonizer, and as he grew older, he completely forgot what it meant to belong to land.

The twin of Distance was called Dominance, and Dominance not only wanted to get as far from home as he could; he wanted to conquer, to pillage, to burn. Joyless he was, this sad son, and he took out his motherless rage on slow-living farmers and mountain dwellers.

The fourth son born to the good king was called Speed. Speed never stopped moving and thinking and running. Speed never stopped to see the way the winter sun cast the alder bark in such strange light or to feel the spring wind on his skin. He missed omen after omen this way, and his insides shook so that he never slept.

The fifth son, the last wormy acorn, was called Separateness, and a tragic beast he was. Separateness believed he was alone, that he belonged to nothing. Separateness was always cold, forever shivering in his isolation and eternally broken by his bone-deep belief that we all live and die alone.

Now, the king, as I said, was no fool. He did not want his sad sons to rule. He knew what would become of the land he loved if these fearsome five were allowed to lead, but he also knew that any king had to be initiated by me, Maeve. He remembered the six trials he himself had to pass when he was young, and he was comforted knowing his sons would never pass such tests. The stone of destiny would not sing for them — he was sure of it — so, when his time came to die, he worried very little for the fate of his kingdom. He named a new king who was not of his blood, who loved this land that was me and would surely continue to rule fairly and revere the spirits of the soil.

Of course, his terrible sons had other plans. I watched, you know. I watched when the five sons called Greed, Distance, Dominance, Speed, and Separateness slaughtered the king their father had chosen and claimed rulership themselves. They had no right. Do you hear me? They had no right to rule. It was never destined. Never divined. They were never supposed to rule.

Kingdoms rose and fell while these angry orphans wore their stolen crowns. Generations upon generations lived and died. The old ways were forgotten, the old stories hidden, the rivers poisoned and the mountains mined, and those who still remembered me, those who refused to bow to these monsters, were killed. I, the initiator of kings, was cast out, so an outcast I became.

I, Maeve — I, Goddess — walked the land as a leper, a shunned and shamed hag with flaking skin and the most righteous rage in her red eyes. It seemed hopeless for so long; it seemed as if all was lost. It seemed these tragic sons would rule forever. People said things like "This is just the way it is," and more of my hair would fall to the ground. People stopped praying to me and loving the land, and my finger bones grew brittle and crumbled to dust. I was without hope for a long, long time.

I was a forgotten matriarch with flaking skin.

Then an apocalyptic something struck the world. An inexplicable cosmic shift that I'd like to take credit for, but I cannot. This was not the gods. There was a storied intelligence afoot, you see, a grander design that found these five angry orphan kings — kings who had ruled so long they thought themselves gods — with their defenses down. They'd become far too confident in their power, you see.

This is the moment your world finds itself in right now.

The angry orphan sons called Greed, Distance, Dominance, Speed, and Separateness are all sitting around the campfire in an oak grove getting drunk, and I, the leprous Goddess with the long memory, am watching them from the shadows and waiting for some unknown sign that it's time. A sign, a plague, a cosmic moment that says now.

Now is the time.

And you know what I did? I seduced those fools even as the cracked and crumbling creature they made me be. Even as leper, the Goddess has a lure even the most poisonous predator cannot refuse. They still longed for me, you know, and I took them, one by one.

I took Separateness into the forest, and I held him to my scarred breast, and I pressed my cracking lips to his skin, and I told him he was not alone. I tied him to the belly of a mother wolf and let her suckle him like a motherless pup.

I took Speed into the forest and bade him walk so slowly he wept. I froze his tongue so he couldn't speak, and I bound him to the oak tree that bore him.

I seduced Dominance by telling him he'd rule forever, and then I whipped him with a hawthorn branch; then I lured Distance into the deep river and locked him down with stones to keep him right there in place until he remembered the songs of the land, until he could hear the hymns of the salmon and the bear.

I saved Greed for last, you know. I let him think he could have me. I, the Goddess, the great prize. I, the divine treasure piece, the one missing jewel in his crown. Then I buried him from the neck down in the wild earth, and I showed him all he could never have. I showed him all that was unownable, and I told him property was illusion. I lifted the veil from his eyes, and he wept with his whole body under that ground that was me.

He's still weeping now. Can you hear him?

He weeps for what he's done even now, when the flesh has fallen from his bones and a single solstice heather flower grows from his barren eye socket. Even now, when the Witches of the world are singing soft skin back onto my bones and drinking with me. Even now, when the world is regreening itself and the time of the Great Remembering has begun.

Some say the gods left these waters long ago, but I say the waters are god. I, Maeve, say we are still here. Sing for me. Drink with me. Sing for me. Drink with me. Drum for me. Dance with me. Howl with me.

Rise to your feet and hear me while this blood river rises around my thighs. Swim with me. The final stage in your initiation is upon you, and it is a ritual bath, a sacred baptism in the mythic waters. Come. Strip yourself of all that binds. Release yourself from all the vows you did not take. Remember you are built from stars. Hold the tension of this knowing and bathe with me.

I am flaming-haired justice and the hex come to pass. I am a Goddess of destruction and a living reminder that all worlds exist at once. I am toxic to reason. I poison the rational. I drown the old and crumbling ways in blood. I cast those angry orphans who hide behind their weapons into the dust. I am the protectress of the wildest children screaming their truths in the streets, and I am not leaving.

If you are not just reading but tasting these words, you have been chosen. Be deviant. Be monster. Slither around the fringes of this imploding golden fortress like a knowing serpent-queen. Become the long-horned beast of heathen desire, the Queen of Holy Intoxication you've always been.

Is that you, Maeve?

Is that you?

Is that you?

Some say the gods left these waters long ago, but I say the waters are god. I, Maeve, say we are still here. Sing for me.

❧ *Guiding Story Remembrances* ❧

Feel free to answer any or all of these queries in symbols rather than words, finishing your artful invocation that begins your Book of Water.

1. How do you relate to the Queen of Holy Intoxication's energy? How do you see her?
2. When have you been this queen?
3. What feels like your truest form in those fleeting moments when you feel the strongest kinship with the sacred waters of this pleasure planet?
4. What else did this story lantern illuminate for you?

Opening Spell: Sipping from the Heathen Queen's Goblet

This is a small spell of naming your desires. Find a vessel, a cup, that speaks the language of beauty to you. Fill it with honey water. (If you are vegan, an alternative might be heather-flower tea or water flavored with the sweetener of your choosing.) Before you drink, whisper into the vessel three desires you hold for the day. Name one for yourself, one for a friend or family member, and one for the global community. Speak these desires clearly in a whisper, in the voice of the heart; then drink this liquid, consuming your named wants and becoming the very essence of what you are invoking. Remember this simple ritual as you move through the creation of your Book of Water. Remember the embodied feeling of consuming, of being fed by, your wants. And so it is.

Water Reflections

To welcome the spirit of the water element is to welcome change. Water might be mist or morning dew, mighty sea or mountain spring. To reflect on the water element is to behold the poetry of our own shifting tides, to name equally holy our moments of solitary initiations by waterfall and lonely bathtub grief ceremonies.

Water teaches us to ebb and flow, to feel into the fallows as much as the fullness, and to permit our senses to be gateways to presence. The Priestess of the Unbridled Sensual archetype is perpetually dancing in the triple rivers of her own fluid pleasures, cyclical creativity, and tidal emotions. We know her when we dance in a rainstorm and welcome the irrational ecstasy of the moment. We name ourselves as her when we surrender to pure presence, yet we know there is a chaotic quality to water. There is power in our sensing flesh; for this reason, we cannot dismiss our ability to feel deeply.

Water Reflection I: The Moving Prayer

"If Earth is the place from which we rise,
if the earth element serves as our ground and our initiation,
then water is our embodied, sensual, moving prayer."

Given a sacred intention, even a single breath might be a prayer. A solitary wander at sunrise might be a moving ceremony, or a meal shared with a loved one so easily becomes a spell of nourishment. Permit a single memory to be an oracle now and ask yourself when you felt your senses were truly holy gateways to the divine. Allow the first memory that bubbles to the surface of your consciousness to gift with you a certain, perhaps unexpected, understanding. If this memory was a snapshot in time, a painting hanging in a gallery, what would you call it? Begin this entry in your Book of Water as follows:

I have a memory alive in my body now, and I've named it...

Now, allowing this memory to be muse, name your "teaching waters." These might be creeks, rivers, vast seas, or claw-foot bathtubs. You may have befriended these waters over many years or encountered their wisdom only once. Name nine "teaching waters," and just as you did for the "teaching lands" in the Book of Earth, grant these waters mythic titles to name them sacred. The mud puddle you played in when you were a child might become the *Babe's Wild Bath*, or the rainstorm you found yourself caught in with a lover might become the *Heathen Storm*. Once you have all nine waters listed in your Book of Water, begin to perceive them as if they are entities. These waters have spirits. What did they teach you?

For each of the nine teaching waters, use the following prompts or create your own:

This water was my teacher, and it was named…
The spirit of this water has a wild look about it, with…
The lesson this water held for me was…

Looking back through your writing, do you notice any words that seem to be precisely the medicine you need right now? Underline these. Look back now on your first memory to which you granted a title — the memory that became muse for this work — and notice if there is a kinship between the words you circled and your memory. Use the title of your memory to complete the first prompt and your underlined words from the "teaching waters" writing to complete the second prompt:

I named the memory [your memory title]
The memory named me [your underlined words]

Water Reflection II: Secret Stories of the Holy Obscene

*"Just for today, let's be Priestesses of the holy obscene.
I've got some tales to tell that are too good to keep secret; let's write
of our debauchery in a new scripture where the verses speak of
hard-nippled freedom and hedonistic revelry. Our parables will be
recited by snickering full-breasted grandmothers after the
little ones are in bed, and our words will be so luscious and vibrant
that they will make the blindly faithful and always pious
question their loyalty to their vengeful gods."*

There are times when secrets are necessary medicine. The secrets we hold sometimes offer us the very quests we need to grant us direction. Of course, there are times when secrets can cause harm to us and others, but there are also occasions when secrets require a timely alchemy. Is there a sweet secret you hold now that feels like it is being slow-cooked in a hidden cauldron somewhere deep in the shadowlands of your psyche? Perhaps it is a secret dream vision or an underground desire? What secret do you hold now that feels ripe and ready to be brought into the light? Grant this secret a title now, beginning this entry in your Book of Water.

I have a secret alive in my body now, and I've named it…

Let this secret be muse and dedicate some verses to its gestation. Envision yourself speaking these verses you are about to write aloud while bathing alone in natural waters, far removed from the judgments and limitations of the everyday. Invite these words to be a foundational invocation for your secret water ceremony, nested somewhere in the yet-to-come.

This secret has always been a quest for…
In this moment, with the healing waters holding me, I know…
To the waters, I release…
From the waters, I welcome…
This moment is a gift, and I receive it with great…

Recall what you titled your initial secret and use this title to complete the first prompt below. Look back on your writing when you are ready and underline repeating and/or potent words. Create a palette of ceremonial water words; then use them to complete the second prompt, concluding this entry in your Book of Water as follows:

I named the secret [your secret's title]
The secret named me [your underlined words]

Water Reflection III: Saved by the Grandmothers

"I am undone. I fall to my knees and am about to claim defeat…
when I feel spectral hands lifting me to my feet. I sense the
grandmothers of my line holding me upright when all I want is to
sink down, and I find the courage to speak of my truest currencies."

Consider the many wisdoms of your lineages. Consider the millennia of art, medicine, songs, and ceremonies housed and hidden in the double-helix sigils of your DNA. Somewhere, in a time long gone and yet, strangely, still here, there is a Witch of your bloodline who is holding a solitary ceremony by a river under a full moon, dreaming of her wild grandchild who will not meet the world for generations to come. What will you call this ancestor?

> *I have an ancestor speaking through me now, and I've named them...*

Feel into this image now and imagine this ancestor speaking a prayer just for you. Imagine them dipping their hands deep in the clear-running water and naming you, their wise and innocent descendant, holy. These are their words to you:

> *To my grandchild, I say...*
> *Always remember that...*
> *When you look to the moon, know...*
> *In your lonelier moments, see me here and sing...*
> *Your memories are my memories, and...*
> *May you dream of me when...*

Recall what you named this ancestor and use this name to complete the first prompt below. Underline the words that repeat and/or feel somehow prophetic or channeled; use these words to complete the second prompt and conclude this entry in your Book of Water.

> *I named the ancestor* [your ancestor's name]
> *The ancestor named me* [underlined words]

Water Reflection IV: Beginning Again

> *"The new moon is a cyclical vow made from the*
> *wild feminine to our heathen souls that whatever missteps*
> *we may have made in our past, whatever wounds have been carved*
> *into our flesh, we can rechristen ourselves with the holy water*
> *of our tears and begin again, at long last."*

Every ending is an initiation. When our world seems to fall into the bone pile, we can look to the dark moon and remember that a new beginning is imminent. Our lives are cyclical, and there is a mythic pattern to every single soul's journey. Choose a life area that feels "stuck" right now, as if it is not moving forward. This perceived immobility does not need to feel bad necessarily, as we do need those times of void and fruition as much as we need the waxing and the waning. You might name a relationship or area of learning, work, health, art, or another domain that feels strangely stagnant. Where do you feel this lack of movement, this "stuckness," in the body? Give it a color, a shape, a location, a temperature, and, last, a name.

I sense a time of shadow here, and I've named it...

Now, look back on the many chapters of your life and ask yourself when this particular life area felt in flow. What were the conditions surrounding this fluidity? When this particular life area was in flow, was there another life area that felt stagnant? While it does not serve us all the time to extract a single life area, a lone character, from the epic myth of our lives, tell the story of this single thing as if it were a fairy tale. Personify this life area as if it were a character in a story. Feel free to alter these prompts as needed:

Once upon a time, there lived a wild...
When the wild one was small, there was much...
At its best, the wild one was surrounded by...
In its depths, the wild one became...
Now, the wild one is in a time of shadow, and it is...

Recall what you named this stagnant time; this will be the answer to the first prompt below. Then return to your writing from the story of the "wild one" and underline the potent words and phrases. Use these to complete the second prompt and conclude this entry in your Book of Water.

I named the time of shadow [your named stagnation]
The time of shadow named me [your underlined words]

Water Spell: Crossing the Threshold

A threshold crossing done with intention is a small initiation, a way of claiming your place in three worlds: the old world, the liminal world, and the new world. There is who you were before you crossed the threshold, who you were when you were between worlds, and who you became. There is before *this* and after *this*.

Find a narrow creek, a shallow river, or a softly running mountain stream. Stand at the water's edge and set the intention to leave something behind. Ask what you are being invited toward. Ask who you are becoming, and ask what old names, roles, beliefs, or ways of being in the world will no longer have space in your reborn psychic landscape. Become an inhospitable environment for these outmoded ways. Leave them behind.

When you feel ready, ask yourself to know the nature of this old skin you are shedding. Where are these dusty beliefs and too-tight roles in the body? What color are they? What shape, and what temperature? Are you ready to leave them behind? If the answer is yes, speak these words while you cross the water, feeling the transformation in the body. Sense the space that is opened when you drop these dead weights, and let every word mark that particular stage of threshold crossing. Be witnessed in this moment by those loving ancestors who have seen such things before, who honor this small ceremony with you and for you.

Before you cross: *I am here, holding the tension of my own becoming. I offer gratitude to who I have been, to the beliefs that served me well, and to the stories that have been mine but are mine no longer.*

As you cross (repeat for the entire crossing): *I am shedding my old skin. I am becoming bones, dropping the dead scales in the water to be carried away by these knowing currents. To the water, I say thank you.*

After you cross: *I am here, and I am reborn into softer flesh. May the road I follow now be full of infinite possibilities, the counsel of wise teachers, and vast opportunities to be innocent and ancient. May I be a living love letter to the Holy Wild. And so it is.*

Water Presences

To be present to the water element is to be present to feeling, to not rush away from the sensations that nourish our feeling flesh, to know the ebb and flow of our lives as continual and holy. To be present to water is to be present to change. When we take our lessons from the rivers and the waves, we see that we are in a continuous process of renewal. We befriend a new abundance here, one attached not to accumulation but to fluidity.

How rich we are in our moments of feeling. How prosperous might we feel if we paid one another in the sound of laughter and song, if we allowed ourselves to meet each moment well. The sound of water is the sound of life. Water is a gift, and our creaturely bodies are made of this wealth.

Water Presence I: An Unbridled Joy

"We must have joy in our Craft."

In our hyperspeed, screen-aglow world, true joy is radical. Joy is akin to the water element because joy will not be hoarded or kept; true joy flows through us, and we must be present to its energy while it lasts. Joy is different from pleasure. Joy is different from contentment or even happiness. Joy is the fleeting sense that our world is meant to sing through us, its most peculiar and creative creatures.

Where do you feel joy in your body? What color is joy? What temperature and shape is joy? How does the energy of joy move within you? If joy were a wild creature, what would this creature look like, and what would its name be? Begin this entry in your Book of Water by naming this creature.

> *I have a creature made of joy alive in my body now, and I've named it...*

If this creature is an embodiment of your joy, how does it spend its days? What rituals grant this creature a felt sense of belonging, and for whom does this creature dance? Tell the story of one day in the life of this joyful creature.

> *The creature crawled from its nest with...*
> *The morning was spent in holy and wild...*
> *By midday, the creature was communing with...*
> *To this creature of joy, time was...*
> *As the sun sank low, the creature laughed out loud at...*
> *At long last, when the darkness came, the creature fell into sleep knowing...*
> *Even its dreams were of...*

Recall the creature's name to answer the first prompt that follows; then underline the repeating words and phrases from the day in the life of your joyful creature to answer the second prompt.

I named the creature made of joy [your creature's name]
The creature made of joy named me [your underlined words]

Water Presence II: The Quieter Side of This World

"I am softening my gaze and looking to the subtle vibrations. I am losing focus on hard edges and bright colors to see the quieter side of the world, and I am bidding the magick to consume me now. I do not fear death. I am the antler-crowned Priestess headed west with a long walking stick and the Mystery packed in her bag."

Our feeling bodies sense far more than we consciously realize. Too often, we seek out blatant signs that our magick is real and ignore the subtle reminders that we belong to a reality that expands well beyond the limits of our ordinary perception. Sometimes we require the dark, the silence, and the stillness in order to sense the Otherworld, but too often our fear of the unknown and centuries of inherited conditioning keep us from listening, prevent us from being held by a deep knowing that we are a single chapter in an epic, ancestral story.

Soften your gaze now. Listen to the many layers of sound in your world. What do you hear? What scents are in the air, and what tastes are on your tongue? Be wholly present now in this moment. Breathe. Invite a knowing to find you here and now, a strange faith that you have tens of thousands of years of ancestors breathing through you, with you, and for you. Sense the lines stretching out in all directions, trusting the grander story of your soul family and your integral role within that tale. Grant a new name now to the cosmic infinite, the grand design, or the more-than-human tale we are all living. The name will not feel perfect; it cannot feel perfect, after all, for our language has yet to evolve to match the beauty of the yet-to-come. Even so, grant what you might call destiny a new name.

I sense a living destiny, and I've named it…

Be present to this moment now, and without editing yourself, complete the following prompts. Let your consciousness stream like a mountain river onto the page. Let the wisdom pour from your heart like waters from a sacred well and become the medicine keeper you searched for when you were younger. Be the wise innocent. Become the holy child of wonder and the hooded knowing hag.

> *In these quiet moments, I see…*
> *There are unseen voices speaking poetry of…*
> *If I listen only to the rhythm of my heart, I feel…*
> *I am becoming…*
> *I am becoming…*
> *I am becoming…*
> *We are becoming…*

Take a few moments before you return to your writing; then underline the words and phrases that stand out as peculiar. Use these words and phrases to answer the second prompt, with the first prompt's answer being your name for destiny:

> *I named the living destiny* [your name for destiny]
> *The living destiny named me* [your underlined words]

Water Presence III:
Benediction to the Forked-Tongued Seductress

"This is my benediction, my body prayer to the forked-tongued
seductress that is me. I'm through with the solemn chants and still-
bodied meditation. My God's skin is made of tree bark, and my Goddess
is not pure. What's more, my friend, my divinity is a genderless spark
that lives and breathes within and without, above and below."

For this practice, if you are able, go to a place where you can sense the wild around you. Lean your back against a tree, or listen to the sounds of a stream. Look to the sky. If you are unable to go to such a place, envision it now in your mind's eye. Begin this entry in your Book of Water by naming this place.

> *I was found by this temple, and I named it…*

Imagine that the growing things here have a memory far longer than any we might call ancient. Imagine that the roots can sense the stories of the land, the stories that stretch back through the realms of deep time. Allow the land, the waters, and the sky to spark the most sacred and extraordinary gratitude within you, and imagine yourself a part of this place. Imagine this place remembering you into being. Be dreamed alive by this place. Become a breathing altar to the Holy Wild. Hold the tension of gratitude in your body while you complete the following prompts, your testament to the enduring and exquisite sacred that surrounds and swaddles us in every *moment*:

> *I came to this place with a heart made heavy by...*
> *A medicine marks me in this moment, an elixir brewed from...*
> *I will a memory to surface now, a memory of me here singing a*
>   *song of...*
> *Time moves strangely in this place, and I think...*
> *When I rest tonight, I will be fed by this moment, and I will*
>   *dream of...*

Notice something new about this place now, a brilliant color or a subtle sound. When you feel ready, return to your writing and underline the key words, words that feel like keys. Reorder them like puzzle pieces. Recall what you named your temple, and complete the following:

> *I named this temple* [your temple's name]
> *This temple named me* [your underlined words]

Water Presence IV: Spells as Conversation

"Every spell she casts is an affirmation, and a loud one at that,
of the kind of world she hopes the future's children
will inhabit wildly and with much joy."

All art is a conversation, and our Witchcraft, our spells, our magick is no exception. We must always consider what we are saying when we cast our spells, knowing that this communication is not limited to the moment we might call "present." A spell requires a softening of linear time's grasp, and by extension, the conversation we have with the world through our spellwork reverberates through the many layers of time like a voice rippling through water.

Name yourself word-witch now and write a spell for the yet-to-come. Whatever season you are in, sense a version of you who is living a joyful moment in the season to come. If you are in the heat of summer, write of yourself dancing beneath the harvest moon. If you are shrouded in the dark of winter, write of yourself walking under the budding trees of spring. First, feel this moment with all your senses as if it is a snapshot in time. What will you call this vision? Begin this entry in your Book of Water as follows:

I see a living vision, and I've named it...

Now, describe this moment in as much detail as you can, holding the tension of joy while you write this vision real.

Here I am, full of an unnameable joy that dances through me like...
Here I am, beneath a moon of...
Here I am, hearing...
Here I am, tasting...
Here I am, feeling so...
I remember writing of this moment on that strange day when...
Now, it is here, and I understand...
There is an ancient ancestor witnessing me in this moment, and I know...
There is a loving descendant witnessing me in this moment, and to them, I say...

Recall what you named the vision and read back through your writing. Underline the words and phrases that feel channeled or perfectly bizarre, the parts of your vision that feel real. Know that this vision longs for you as much as you long for it, and complete the following concluding prompts:

I named the living vision [your name for the vision]
The living vision named me [your underlined words]

❧ *Water Spell: Wedding the River* ❧

Water is precious. To be a conscious human in these times is to honor the value of water. Depending on your ancestry, recent generations of your lineage may have forgotten that water is a treasure, may have taken water for granted and exploited or polluted the many streams and vast oceans that nourish us, but you have water-revering ancestors if you trace your lines back far enough. We are tasked now to rekindle a romance with water, to protect and cherish the wells.

Choose a watery place you are willing to wed. This is no small decision, of course, especially if you live a nomadic life of movement. Is there a body of water you might call lover? Ideally, this is a place you can visit for the ceremony, but if distance or other circumstances preclude you from standing at the edge of these waters you will wed, know that there is a part of you who is there, hearing the poetry of the waves or the songs of the stream.

When you are ready, adorn yourself and go to the water, if only energetically. Stand in or near this sacred spring, creek, river, or other liquid sanctuary. Breathe. Speak truth. You may use the words I offer here or write your own vows.

On this, the day of all days, I wed these waters. I am bride to sea. I will love, honor, protect, and cherish these precious, precious currents.

I am a living vow. May my blood run in rhythm with these waters. May my tears make their way to the sea.

May no harm come to these waters. May the ancestors of my bloodlines who knew the sanctity of water stand with me and the spirits of this place. As one circle, we shield these waters. As a heathen bride to sea, my soul shall swim here from now until forever.

And so it is.

Water Visions

To gaze into the well, to scry the yet-to-come in dark waters, is an ancient practice. Our bodies are mostly made of water, so perhaps the truest mirror is made of this sacred element. What we see in water, what we glean from a softly rippling reflection, could never be apparent in a stone or a flame.

Have you ever stared so long at a swift-running creek that you began to see the whole of your ancestral lines dancing in the currents? Have you heard the voices of your forebears in the hush of waves cresting? We are born in water and from water; for this reason, our Water Visions speak to our homecoming.

Water Vision I: Art from the Fertile Dark

"The fertile dark all artists draw from when they birth something new into being is essentially pure, primeval creatrix energy; there is no valid separation between the sensual and the creative..."

It is a radical act to make art for art's sake, to not bind the value of the *making* to the price of the *made*. Our art, like our spellwork, is made better by our tending to the fertile void, by pausing long enough to listen to the spirit of what will be born of our hands, our voice, and our vision. There is a word that wants to be written by you and you alone. There is an image that wants to be born to the world, but it can come only through you.

Look to the patterns you find in your art, whatever your art may be, and see what story those patterns create. If a pattern does not reveal itself to you immediately, allow this darkness to be part of the process. When you feel ready, name the particular art you create; let this be a secret name for now. Tell no one. Let it be a different name from any you have used before in your sacred work, and begin this entry in your Book of Water.

> *I have a strange and holy art that comes only through me, and I've named it...*

Begin now to envision how you might more fully tend to the fires of your creativity. The rivers of feeling, the sacred flows of sensuality and emotionality, run swiftly toward our creative fires to feed our artistic expressions. Imagine your holiest art as a lone flame eternally burning with the essence of your unique genius. The container for this flame — the canvas, the garden, the casserole, the ceremony, the poem, or whatever form your art tends to take — can never be perfect. It is impossible for the available vessels we might find for our art to fit the magnitude of our souls' gift, our reason for being. This is why the books and the songs we might write never feel complete; they can't, because they aren't.

Even so, we keep going. We keep asking ourselves how we can best show the flame to the world, to those who care to see it. Describe this flame as best you can, knowing that our language is often insufficient when it comes to describing those deep wells of powers we might call purpose.

In my quietest moments, I can sense a lone flame burning in the name of…
The fuel for this fire is…
In its light, I scry…
If I show this flame to the more-than-human world, I am witnessed by…
My greatest fear lives in the shadows around this flame, and it is called…
In the flame's light, I am fearless, and I know…
Before I take my last breath, I vow to let this flame…

If you feel called, gather art materials of your choosing and create imagery, however abstract, that reflects the warmth of this flame back to you. The first prompt below is your name for your holy art. When you are ready, underline the words and phrases that feel potent from your writing, and stitch together an end to the second prompt.

I named this holy art [your name for your holy art]
This holy art named me [your underlined words]

Water Vision II: The Liminal Space of Creation

"Come inside, and permit me to pour you something earthen
and bitter before I tell you of my dream vision, before I ask
you to question all you know to be true, and before I bid you cast
your sweet psyche into the liminal space between the only-imagined
and the very real yet-to-come. Here, let me hold your hands.
Breathe softly and sink your consciousness down to the womb-heart,
down to that energetic void between life and death.
There, time knows no bounds."

As orphans of modernity, our spirits can so easily become constrained by the limits of linear time. We speak of the scarcity of time; there's *never enough* time, we shouldn't *waste* time, we need to *make more* time. The language we use when we talk of time shows us how flawed our perspective is when we think of time as a finite commodity. For everyone, though, there are certain practices that allow time to move differently, that invite even the most tightly scheduled day to breathe a bit more freely.

Of course, it is a great privilege to befriend time in this way. The landscape of every life will not allow for the strange choreography of time stretching to take place regularly and often, but the medicine of what the Irish might call *eternal time* is available to all. A little bit of deep time's medicine goes a long way. Take a moment now to breathe, to imagine you are breaking the cage of linear time around every cell in your body; then consider the practices you engage in that make time seem to bend. You know these because when you reenter linear time, when the painting is finished or long wander is complete, you see that far more hours have passed than you realized. Name your experience of deep time now:

> *I can sense deep time when it is close, and I've named it…*

Imagine how the span of your day would feel if you could spend it immersed in the practices that bring you closer to deep time, the gardening or the fire tending. These practices might be what you would call your art. They are usually goalless and solitary but not always so. Describe a day in the life of *you*, living a little closer to deep time's dance, engaging in the practices that bring you a greater sense of beingness.

> *I woke marked by a simplicity I cannot name, and I lay there*
>   *wondering…*
> *I brewed myself a cup of…*
> *I don't know how long I stood there, just…*
> *Before I knew it, I was making…*
> *I wandered…*
> *I became…*
> *I sang a song of…*
> *I rested in a deeper understanding of…*

When you feel ready, underline the medicinal words and phrases; then use your name for deep time to complete the first prompt below, and stitch the underlined words and phrases together to complete the second prompt.

I named deep time [your name for deep time]
Deep time named me [your underlined words]

Water Vision III: Witch of the Waves

"This eerie night belongs to me, and I will bid all matrilineal blessings to wash ashore and keep me warm. My desire and my art are holy, and these last long nights I have fed both with underwater soul-food and much sex-to-spirit fusion."

The sea is an ancient sorceress. Everyone can feel the rhythm of waves inside their bellies. In the Celtic cosmology of land, sea, and sky, the sea is the realm of the ancestors, the underworld, the deep medicine. In *The Smell of Rain on Dust*, Martin Prechtel writes: "A stretch of sea coast with no people is such a capable healer of loss and all types of wounds." In the great gray depths, the sea can hold it all, the sorrow and the joy, the grief and the gratitude.

Imagine yourself now sitting on a stony beach. Imagine the rhythm of your breath matching the pulse of the waves. Look to the horizon where sea meets sky, and call on a timeless sort of peace to find you, to hold you. Name this vision now as if it were a masterpiece hung in a gallery, and allow that artful name to begin this entry in your Book of Water.

I sense a seascape in my dreams, and I've named it...

Become word-witch now and envision what might have brought you to this water's edge. Write the story of *you*, having begun a great journey that ended just here, held by sand, sea, and sky.

The day had begun like any other, but so soon I realized...
I wasn't looking for it, but I was found by the great...
I left my home in search of...

On the way, I met many creatures who…
In the forest by the sea, I found…
I shed the many masks that…
I took a new name, a name of…
I baptized myself in the salty waters of…
There, at long last, I rested, looking long into the horizon and
  knowing…

Take a breath. Recall what you named the vision of you there, nested on the shore. Let this be the answer to the first prompt below. Underline the words and phrases that call out to you from the remaining writing; then reorder the language as you see fit to complete the second prompt, concluding this entry in your nearly complete Book of Water.

I named this seascape [your seascape's name]
This seascape named me [your underlined words]

Water Vision IV: Water and Reclamation

"Water will cleanse away what no longer belongs, purify and name
our darkness, and support our reclamation of sensual freedom."

We know, though we often forget, that our bodies are mostly water. There's a reason why water rituals exist across all cultures, lands, and spiritual paths. Water is life. Water is medicine. Water washes the body after death and the babe after birth.

In the wake of climate collapse, our holy waters are being threatened, polluted, desalinated, and exhausted. Modernity does not respect the waters, and the wilds are forced, again and again, to pay the infinite and unsustainable price of civilization. Imagine yourself now near a body of water close to where you live; it can be a creek or a sea. See the vision and hear the rhythm of this place now, as it is home to sacred waters. Grant this place a mythic name:

I was found by these sacred waters, and I named this place…

Write a healing blessing for these waters now. Afford this practice the attention it deserves. Venerate what we so often take for granted.

To you, the holy and wild waters of…
I am your child, and I am singing you a soft song of…
I hold an ache for you in my heart, and it feels…
Even now, I see a vision of you with…
The children of the yet-to-come will know…
Beneath this moon, I pray for your…
So clearly do I see…

If you feel called, read your writing aloud in that place. Feel the waters of your blood be changed in response to your vows. Gather any waste that does not belong in or around the waters, and offer gratitude to the water spirits for witnessing you. Recall what you named this holy place and let that name be the answer to the first prompt below. Underline the strong words and phrases from your water blessing, and use those to complete the second prompt.

I named the sacred waters [your name for the hallowed water]
The sacred waters named me [your underlined words]

 ### Water Spell: Visions from the Well

Water scrying is an ancient practice. The hooded grandmothers looked in the well for answers. The seers divined in the mountain spring. Even if you have never water-scried before, there is a part of you that remembers this practice. It is bone memory. Begin by discerning a particular life area that feels in transition, that you would like to seek clarity on.

Fill a dark bowl or pot with water. Find a small stone that you feel somehow mirrors the life area in transition. Hold the stone in both hands and begin to repeat these words: *I know what I must know. I see what I must see. I hear what I must hear. I am who I must be.* When the stone feels charged by your words, place it in the water.

Create sacred space now. Face the north. Call your loving ancestors of the north, past and future, to come closer to your circle and witness you. *To the north, to my seer ancestors, to the sacred energies of the Earth, I say welcome.* Face the east. Call your loving ancestors of the east, past and future, to come closer to your circle and witness you. *To the east, to my seer ancestors, to the sacred energies of the air, I say welcome.* Face the south. Call your loving ancestors of the south, past and future, to come closer to your circle and witness you. *To the south, to my seer ancestors, to the sacred energies of the fire, I say welcome.* Face the west. Call your loving ancestors of the west, past and future, to come closer to your circle and witness you. *To the west, to my seer ancestors, to the sacred energies of the waters, I say welcome.*

Return to the chant now. Keep your gaze fixed on the stone and repeat these words: *I know what I must know. I see what I must see. I hear what I must hear. I am who I must be.* Let the chant anchor your gaze. You can move your body, but do not take your gaze from the stone. Your mind will get loud; let it. Keep chanting and gazing.

Soon, what we might call the "optical illusions" will appear; there might suddenly be two stones or more, you could see strange colors, or the whole vessel may seem to suddenly levitate. Let all of this happen, and keep going. Keep chanting and gazing for at least twenty minutes.

The "shift in consciousness" will be obvious when it happens. You will suddenly feel something akin to a deeper connection with this water, with this stone, with this practice as a whole. Some describe it as love or general belonging. When you feel this, it is time to divine your message.

What do you see there in the water? What do you hear? Close your eyes when it feels right, and notice what you see behind the lids. You may not know exactly what the answer means in this moment, but you do have an answer. This might be "blue star" or "yellow bird." Set the intention to know the meaning of the symbol within three days; ask for a dream to gift you with the final clarity.

Open the circle by offering gratitude to the ancestors and elements from west to south to east to north. Place your hands on the ground. Breathe from low in the belly. Notice where you are with all your senses. Come back to ground. What do you hear, see, smell, and feel? What tastes are on your tongue? Go for a wild walk and ponder your answer. Release the water to the land with gratitude, and place the stone on your altar. And so it is.

Testament to Water

Write your second Heathen Testament now, your Testament to Water. Begin by writing an invocation to the water element. You may use the prompts I offer here or create your own:

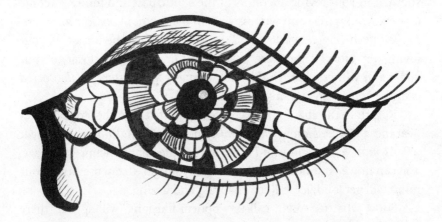

This is my testament of sea, stream, and rain, and I am baptizing myself in the name of…
I am asking unanswerable questions of…
To the water, I say…

Go back through your Water Reflections, Presences, and Visions, and look to the last line from all twelve journal entries. Stitch these together to become your "Water Verses":

Verse 1: The memory named me…
Verse 2: The secret named me…
Verse 3: The ancestor named me…
Verse 4: The time of shadow named me…
Verse 5: The creature made of joy named me…
Verse 6: The living destiny named me…
Verse 7: The temple named me…
Verse 8: The living vision named me…
Verse 9: Deep time named me…
Verse 10: My holiest art named me…
Verse 11: The seascape named me…
Verse 12: The sacred waters named me…

Complete the final prompt below. Then read your Testament to Water aloud in a sacred place, and if possible, follow the reading with a time of silence. Be witnessed by your ancestors. Be held by the water. And so it is.

I am here, held by the waters, and I know…

Possible Additions to Your Book of Water

- Use watercolors to create thirteen "spell paintings," one for each moon of the year. Allow the colors you use to represent something you wish to invoke, to call into your world at that particular time, for that specific season. Let the creation of the painting be a spell in itself, and then use your art as a divination tool. What do you see if you stare long into these peculiar shapes and shades?
- Create a body-prayer ritual for removing obstacles to creative flow. What songs inspire you? Make a list. How will you adorn yourself? What time of day might you move through this ceremony? How will you create sacred space and shake these blockages loose?
- Write a prayer to an ancestor who might resource you in your art. You may know them by name or they may be nameless, but know that we all have a loving, supportive spirit, one of our beloved dead, who was able to create fearlessly. How might you pray to them when you are immersed in a project? Let this prayer be poetry. Honor them through your words.

Book Three

The Book of
FIRE

Heathen Verses of the Burning Temple

*L*ike all the elements, the fire element holds the power to give both life and death. Nature does not abide by our notions of morality, and fire grants us lifesaving warmth as easily as it causes destruction. Rage, will, and magick are similar forces in that they are not necessarily "good" or "bad"; their effect depends on the one who wields them.

To create a kinship with the fire element means to respect your own power, to not shy away from your own heat, and to be clear about your intentions when the flames are kindled. A fire left untended is dangerous, we know. A fire started without a conscious choice of location, fuel, and plan to douse the flames if necessary can mean death, but with such considerations, a fire might mean life.

As you write your Book of Fire, do so from the place of ferocity and passion. Look to the stories of those Goddesses of destruction from the traditions in which you work, those death bringers and storm riders. Let your words get so hot that you have to take a step back from time to time. Leave nothing unrisked.

Word-Spell: Songs from the Pyre

The wind's teeth were sharp on this fated evening when the bone-women were dancing all around my humble forest altar of stone. I set my mind toward the fire, even so. The season of shadow was looming, my tears were falling, and I welcomed this small death with a haunting hum and a gift of my hair.

With care, with song, I plucked a long-burning and star-shaped ember from my heart and named it the fire seed. I fed it with a slow breath and pine dust. I softened into this moment by chanting all the names that were once mine but were mine no longer, and the budding blaze swallowed them like dead leaves.

The smoke started rising, and I stoked this altar fire with the sound of my drum. I placed a fallen branch in the flames, and I named it tyranny. I tied three twigs together and named them greed, power hunger, and negligence. My drum grew louder. My dance grew bolder, and the fire rose higher and higher still.

I became pyromancer and fire dancer. In the sharp-tongued flames, I saw a wild hag singing for innocence. I saw a weaver-woman stitching the world whole, and I saw a child-king lay his crown in the mud and run to the sea. The three became one then, and I saw them grow antlers like a stag. I stared into the black-mirror pool of their eyes, and just there, I saw myself without skin.

Skull-faced, I was. Fleshless and feasting on these visions, I became ravenous for prophecy. I was the Mother of Babylon risen from her unmarked grave, and I was every burned healer and hunted Witch. I was the scorned wild embodied in bones, and I howled. I howled for the ravaged lands and the rising seas. I howled for every unhealed wound, for every unspoken truth and every forgotten babe. My bones shattered into a million shards, and I was a splintered heap of bloodied ivory pins smoldering in the fires of my own making.

I became a pile of ash and bone, and I rested there for a time. I rested while the coals cooled and the wind died. I rested while the thunder rolled in from the west, and I rested when the rains came speaking in the rhythm of resurrection. I was the Holy Wild returned with a soft heartbeat pulsing under broken ribs, and I was rising once more, softly, slowly, one pulse beat at a time.

To Begin Your Book of Fire: An Artful Invocation

Begin your Book of Fire by drawing an image of your inner hearth, the always-burning altar that keeps you going even when the grief is great, that stays alight even in the midst of consuming darkness. What does your inner altar reveal about you? Hold the tension of this image. Be warmed by it. Feel the heat of purpose.

Allow each of the following questions to then spark more imagery, symbols, or words. Fill your page with your strange responses to these queries, surrounding the inner-hearth image with your nonanswers. Take a moment to honor this, the birth of the spirit of your Book of Fire; then move through each of the twelve journal entries at your own pace, in your own time.

What or whom are you willing to fight for? Why?

What do you know for sure you believe in?

Who are your heroes? What traits do they possess?

What is the secret name of your inner warrior?

What are the patterns visible in your spiritual transformations?

Story Lantern: The Ire of the Fallen Mother

Read this story spell aloud if you feel called. Let it be a guiding lantern illuminating precisely what you need to know now, today, as you read these words. Add any images the story sparks or words from the story that feel potent to your artful invocation that begins your Book of Fire.

Some say the gods left these fires long ago, but I say the fires are god. I, the fallen mother, say we are still here. Sing for us.

Let our stories not be caged in that prison called the past. Let your hope for a peaceable world not be trapped on that unreachable icy apex called future. Do not dare hear my story. I, Macha, ask you: Is it sufficient to merely hear the wilds? Is it medicine enough to passively receive poetry poured deep into the soul?

No, do not dare hear my story. Meet my story, and meet it well. Smell the strange brew of my salt-iron blood as it flavors the mud and the moss. Lick at my skin and taste the raw wet of a dead mother's tears. Gnash your teeth and rage with me. Touch the rain-slick coat of the horses who carried my shredded body home, and if you hear anything, hear the guilt-heavy gasps of the cursed warriors who watched me die.

Do not hear my story. Fall on your knees, howl, and claw at this ground that is my grave. I, the fallen mother, am still here. Dig for my bones and lie with me. Cradle and rock my skull with a gentleness I have missed so dearly. Press those warm and living lips of yours to this cold, stained ivory and sing.

I, Macha, am in need of my own ferocious fire-keeper, and today, that flame tender is you.

Meet this story now, as you would meet god in the ground, and sing. My story is a sharp one, and it is not for everyone. Hold the mythic image of wild horses running free on a storm-torn beach while you meet my story; let this image bring you a cooling solace when my story burns.

I was a Goddess of the Wilds, and that is all you need know. These mountains were my throne, these forests my altars, these caves homes to my many secrets. The sea was my distant grandmother, and even the gods grow lonely.

Even the gods long for the weight of time, for the container of flesh and the warmth of blood. The longing passes, of course, but sometimes the cords of fate find a reluctant god and yoke them to a grief-filled home. Sometimes, the destinies of a lonely god and a lonelier mortal hum so loudly with a deafening synchronicity, and all parties become choiceless.

Such was the way I met my husband.

The desire for that particular ache only humans feel became so great, and I know this is hard to understand. The human experience is so bound to duality, and humans live between the extremes of pleasure and pain, joy and sorrow. The depths of grief make the heights of ecstasy all the greater, and this is something the gods cannot know until they take mortal form.

I wanted the scent of the sea to burn my nose. I wanted to run so swiftly against an October rain that the drops marked my skin, and I did not know it, but at the precise midnight moment when my longing had never been greater, there was a farmer wailing in anguish over the loss of his woman and his son.

So great was his grief, so sharp my desire, that fate tied our destinies together in a sudden and irrevocable knot.

I found myself weary and heavy with flesh and bone. I, Macha, found myself in a mortal body, a heart-drum pounding in my ears and a slow-walking, bemuscled horse between my thighs. The land reeked of death, and a spectral keening rang shrill over the mountains. These familiar wilds were a death song, and I was a red-cloaked banshee come to carry a soul home.

My journey became a sin eater's prayer, and I hummed low and soft to the rhythm of my beast's footsteps. I knew no regret, even as the storm rolled over the mountain. I repented nothing, even as the chill started to take me. I was ready for whatever fate would come for me, and fate did come for me.

A lone and humble home dug into a hillside called to me, and I knew this place. It smelled of burning peat and blood even through the rain, and what I thought was thunder was the sound of a man in mourning. I met my mortal husband there beneath the thick shroud of rain clouds, rocking the body of his oldest son as the fever cooked him.

There's something about weeping men, is there not? They move between despair and rage in a single breath. Their leather-skinned bodies shiver, and they become something more, something whole, something wild. This was how I found the farmer, flanked by the ghosts of his dead. His spectral wife stood at his side and beckoned me to come closer, pleaded with me to bring warmth to her home again, to save the life of her man. His living babes huddled around the fire, mother-hungry and covered in filth.

I want to say I stayed because I took pity on these grieving creatures, but in truth, this home was already mine before I arrived. The human tears, the soulless body, the storm, the fire; this was the fecund muck the gods long for, and I was home.

I said nothing to him. I let him mourn. So in his depths was he that he did not speak, though he would tell me later he thought me a Goddess of the Underworld come to collect his boy.

I stoked the fire hotter. I cleaned his babes. I killed, skinned, and cooked a rabbit, all while he wept. I sang his living ones to sleep with the songs of the gods, and he fell silent.

The rain had ceased; the house was warm and smelled of meat. Hours had passed since my arrival, and the first words the farmer spoke to me were barely a whisper. He spoke into the skin of his son, and he said, "Stay. Woman, will you stay? I know not what you are, but do not leave me."

And I, Macha, stayed.

Only a year had passed, and I found myself still there in that home, an October storm brewing over the mountains, skinning a rabbit. The farmer's son's and woman's ashes had long since ridden away on the wind, but his other babes, nearly talking, were fed and fat, alive and well. My own belly was full with child, and soon our house would be filled with the soft mewling sounds of my very own innocent flesh and blood. I, Macha, was to be mother. I would nurse a babe at my breast. I would smell of milk, and I would sing lullabies of horses and the sea.

Some say the gods left these fires long ago, but I say the fires are god. I, the fallen mother, say we are still here. Sing for us.

The farmer loved me well, and our home was a slow and simple place. I had never known such joy. The gods know nothing of the creaturely bliss that comes from falling asleep in the arms of another or eating the food grown on the land where you live. The gods know nothing of this, but I came to love that feeling flesh of mine, that tenderhearted man of mine.

Some say I was fooled. Some say I was a fallen angel, but I know I was human by choice.

This home, this man, these babes were mine, I thought, and right then, right at that moment, an unnatural sound pulled me from my work. The raven lay dead without a mark outside my door, a red-berried rowan branch in its beak. Not a feather was amiss on the corvid, as if it had fallen right out of the sky midflight, and I knew this omen to mean death.

My husband was leaving that day for the king's feast, and I begged him to stay. I begged my man to decline the invitation, to resist the urge to drink and eat with the so-called noblemen of the land. I told him of the raven, and he understood, but he went anyway.

As he cradled me and shushed me like a petulant child, I knew, in that moment, this would be the last time I was held in love by my husband.

"Do we not have a good life?" I asked him as he mounted my horse. "Why do you do this?"

"My love —" he started, and for the first time since I'd come to this place, something of my god nature swelled within me, and the babe in my belly stirred. My skin grew hot as hellfire, and my red hair writhed in the wind like flames.

"Hear me, husband. You will not speak of me to others. You will not tell them you have a wife. If you do not keep this secret, I swear it, you will lose all you have come to love."

I turned and left him as the rains began to fall, and I prepared myself for what I knew was coming.

Three days passed, and the moon was full. I was beginning to sense not one but two babes inside me, and I thought about leaving. I did. I thought about taking the babes and heading into the mountains. I knew how to live on this land. I was this land, and still, I did not leave.

The king's guards came for me in the moonlight, and I saw the ghost of the farmer's wife in the field as I rode off between the stone-faced men, two babes wrapped to my back and two others stirring within my womb, pressing against my bones.

The journey was long, and one of the guards gave the illusion of kindness.

"I'm sorry about this, lady. If I can help you, I will," he said, but when the time came, when I needed someone to come to my aid, he did not. His words were empty. He told me my husband had been drunk and bragging about the otherworldly beauty and unnatural speed of his wife. "He said you were not of this world," the guard told me, and I could tell he agreed with my fool of a husband. "You are to race the king's horses, as a matter of sport, and all the men of this land will be watching."

My babes stirred, the living and the unborn, and I saw the fate that would befall me well before we approached the king's grounds. I moaned, and my labor began. I leaned on the guard as he brought me to stand before the king; then I, a Goddess turned human, begged.

They took my husband's children to him, and I saw in his face the same lament I saw the night we met. I begged for the race to be postponed. I wailed. I saw the women in the crowd appeal to their husbands to stand up to the king. I saw them hold their own bellies when my pains came, and I saw them feel what I felt, but the men did nothing. The men of this land that was me did nothing.

My waters broke. My god ire was up, mixing with all the ferocity of a wolf mother, and I spit at this vile monster who called himself king. He asked my name, and I snarled, "My name and the names of my children will be given to this place."

The winds howled then, and I knew this moment had been scripted. I was without protectors, and fate alone had found me here. We all have moments such as this, do we not? We all find ourselves part of what we know to be a larger story, a story within many other stories, the smallest of an infinite number of nesting dolls.

A fire of rage sparked to life under my ribs. The race began, with me, a mother in labor, racing against a king's chariot. I, Macha, howled and ran, spitting vitriol across the whole expanse of field. Many miles did I run. I was the fire, and the fire was me. I ran my body to death. I won the race to the sound of weeping women, and my flesh fell heavy to the ground in exhaustion just as my babes erupted from between my bloodied legs; their lifeless faces were the last vision I saw as a mortal, and I cursed the men of this land who stood by and did nothing while the god-mother of these mountains they called home was forced to run for the amusement of a king.

I, Macha, cursed them to be stricken with the pains of childbirth for five days and five nights when their strength was most needed. I cursed their sons' sons' sons for nine generations forward. I cursed them from the ethers as I watched my fool husband weep over the body of yet another woman he loved, and I cursed him, too, even as I watched him clean and wrap the bodies of our dead children and gift the three of us to the land, this land that was me.

Some say the gods left these fires long ago, but I say the fires are god. I, the fallen mother, am still here. Sing for us.

I say the mothers are still weeping and watching me run, and I say my children's ghosts are lovingly haunting those who meet my story, who sing to my bones in the ground. I say sometimes ire is good medicine and fire is good poetry.

I, the fallen mother, am still here, making my story heard, weaving this tale with others, leaving a strange mythic tapestry of love, loss, and a rage most righteous in my wake.

I, Macha, am still here. Sing for me.

Guiding Story Remembrances

Feel free to answer any or all of these queries in symbols rather than words, finishing your artful invocation that begins your Book of Fire.

1. What parts of the fallen mother's story, if any, feel like timely lessons for you now?
2. When has your rage been a great and telling teacher?
3. When you create from a place of heat, what form does your art take? What colors, flavors, sounds, or shapes mold your art when it is born in the fires of passion or anger?
4. What else did this story lantern illuminate for you?

Opening Spell: The Oracular Fires

This is a simple but potent spell. Begin by naming a particular passion that feels as if it is cooling. This is an art, a project, a relationship, or a way of being in the world that you want to feel some heat around but that seemingly has gone cold. Find a strong stone that, in some way, reflects this cooled thing back to you. Try not to overthink it. When you feel ready, safely set a small fire to burn, and place the stone in the flames. Keep it contained. Be vigilant. When the ashes cool, pull your stone from the fire and see what you see. What lessons does the stone have for you? Scry a vision in this stone. Let it become teacher. Keep the stone on your altar as you write your Book of Fire, and visit this wise teacher often. Track any new knowings or evolving understandings around what the burned rock is showing you. And so it is.

Fire Reflections

Fire promotes reflection. Even the ancients understood the merit of staring long into the flames and finding solace there. The fire shows us how we have endured countless struggles, the childhood battles that ended long ago but we continue to fight, and the many rough places that let us see how resilient we truly are.

The heart of every home used to be the hearth. In some parts of the world, to allow the winter fire to die meant death. Despite the conveniences of modernity, our souls still understand the importance of a fire built well, the sacred communion that occurs when a hungry spirit sits in silence with the flames, and the profound revelations that come when we turn off our small screens and let the fire speak.

Fire Reflection I: The Ancestral Fire

"For our ancestors, fire was the center point of communal gathering,
a place to nourish the soul with food, warmth, and conversation.
A place to dance, mourn, laugh, pray, plot, and dream.
Fire has long been the great and mystical symbol of perpetual hope
amid swelling, cool darkness, a burning promise that this, too,
shall pass and a call to tend the flames with great care
until the dawn ushers in rebirth and renewal."

Fire was the original oracle. Stare into the flames for hours, and you will inevitably scry a deeper knowing of who you are, of where your place is in this wild world of ours. For our ancestors, fire was life. Fire was source, and this wisdom lives in our cells despite our modern conveniences. Recall now a sweeter memory akin to the fire element; this may be a memory of the sunrise, a potent cook fire, or a lone candle lit during a dark hour, or any other memory where flames were present.

What did you show the fire in that moment? Begin this entry in your Book of Fire as follows:

I met the fire, and I showed it…

Now imagine this same memory, but instead of yourself, see an ancestor living this moment, feeling the same emotions you did, perhaps at the same stage of life you were in when the fire marked you. Tell their story now. Let it be part fantasy, part peculiar memory.

The ancestor lit the fire for…
They whispered a prayer of…
They sang a soft song called…
In the dirt, they drew a…
They saw my face then, and they wondered…
To them, I say…

Underline the repeating and powerful words and phrases now. Recall what you showed the fire, how you began this entry in your Book of Fire, to complete the first prompt below. Use your underlined words to stitch together the ending of the second prompt.

I showed the fire [the first piece in this entry]
The fire showed me [your underlined words]

Fire Reflection II: Reclaiming the Flames

"You must reclaim the flames. You must reclaim your right to hope and your right to act, knowing that Witches exist on the fringes of what is acceptable, knowing that the magick keepers have a responsibility to support their core values in their Craft."

A fire is in conversation with the fuel it is burning. The Witch, similarly, is in conversation with their truest currencies, with what they believe their world can become. The Witch understands that any spell of manifestation is also a spell of banishing; when we choose *this*, we are not choosing *that*. There is a flaming ferocity to our discernment, you see, and like a well-lit fire, a spell cannot easily be doused.

Now consider a moment in your life when you truly left behind a way of being in the world that was not yours, when you irrefutably said no to a name, a role, a relationship, or a place. Imagine yourself now, in this moment, locking eyes with that person, with yourself, when you were in the moment of decision. Can you see yourself there in that fateful point in time when you chose the unknown, when you set another version of you to burn? In that moment what were you saying about your fate? Begin this entry in your Book of Fire using the following prompt:

I met my fate, and I showed it…

We often shy away from an understanding of our destined place in this world. It can feel limiting to believe we are here only to serve one particular purpose — to live out one particular genius — or to affirm that there is only one road available to us, that all is written in the stars before we are born. A mature understanding of fate and destiny, however, reveals so much more than a linear journey from birth to purpose. The great storyteller Michael Meade writes in his book *Fate and Destiny*: "Only when seen from the ground of destiny do the suffering and restrictions of an individual life make sense. Fate is purpose seen from the other end of life." Fate is necessarily limiting, but destiny is the path we choose. Destiny is designed by our dance with the world, and we are very much a part of this cocreation.

Take a moment to consider the story of your many choices now, of those many times in your life when you chose one path over another. Are there any apparent patterns in these choices? Perhaps they often occur in autumn or another season, perhaps there seems to be a catalyzing event that precedes these choices, or perhaps there is another common thread that runs through your moments of setting yourself upon a new trajectory. Tell a tale about these moments of choice now, using the prompts I offer here or creating your own:

Once, some may have called me mad, but I knew…
In the days of my innocence, I remember making a choice to…
This choice led me to another, if I'm being honest, and I decided…
When destiny came for me yet again, I chose the road marked with…

I chose...
I burned...
I chose...
I burned...
I chose...
I burned...
In the time of my wisdom, I lastly chose this, to become...

Underline the words that feel particularly important — that stand out to you or feel channeled — and conclude this entry by naming what you showed fate from the initial prompt and stitching together your underlined words:

I showed fate [what you showed fate]
Fate showed me [your underlined words]

Fire Reflection III: You Are the Crucible

"Waste no more time here with me wishing for a quick and
flaming solution; that is their way, not ours. Stop looking to the sky
for a great fireball to smite the mad ones and leave you be.
This is not in the cards, and I am no diamond-bright oracle or
pink-glittery savior. I am the crucible, boiling down the steel out of
which a million-bladed sword will be forged. I am the raging
prophet they tore apart to suit their needs, and you are my hands,
my tongue, and my red-hot still-pulsing guts."

A time comes in our lives when we realize we have become who we needed most when we were younger; this is often a daunting moment because it may feel like there is nowhere left to go, no secret left uncovered or shadowy depth unexplored. Of course, this sense of being trapped at the apex is short-lived, and we begin to feel that the lives we have built for ourselves are a microcosm of the whole, of what we wish for the world. This is not to say we hope everyone becomes just like us or thinks just as we do, but whatever bounty we feel we have harvested, whatever destiny we have chosen, we hope it serves to support the yet-to-come in some way.

Even now, as our climate shifts and crumbles under the weight of colonization and capitalism's unbearable burden, we may feel we have a part to play, a small side role in the epic story of more-than-human evolution. If you are the crucible out of which a brilliant new world will rise — even if this rising occurs long after this current incarnation has ended — tell me, how hot is your fire? What are you putting into this molten container?

Go back and consider a moment of rage now, a moment when you were so angered by a threat to, or betrayal or violation of, something you truly hold dear for the human collective that you were seething. Without feeling the need to embody or sense this anger now, simply see if you can breathe calmly and bear witness to this moment. You are not seeing through the eyes of the person in this memory; rather, you are witnessing this version of you. What were you showing your rage in that moment? Perhaps you were showing your rage it was valued or useful. Perhaps you were showing your rage it could be righteous and valid. If your rage was an entity in that moment, what were you showing this fire creature? Begin this entry in your Book of Fire with the following prompt:

I met my rage, and I showed it...

We rage because we love. The news stories that make us boil do so because we love this world so deeply. In this moment of anger, can you see that you raged because you loved something with a passion that would accept nothing short of rage in the face of its violation? Tell this love story now.

As a child, I fell in love with parts of this world, and they were called...
As a wiser one, I remain enchanted by the...
I love...
I rage when my great love becomes...
I love...
I rage against...
In my sweeter moments, I understand...
In my dream visions, there is no longer...
I will it to be so, this emerging world that seems so distant, so full of...

I am a crucible out of which a new world will rise, and I'm naming this transformation…

Return to the writing and mark the moments that feel loud; use these and the very first prompt from this journal entry to complete the following:

I showed my rage [what you showed your rage]
My rage showed me [your underlined words]

Fire Reflection IV: The Earth Bride

"With this blood, I thee wed. I am painting my face with worm-riddled loam and tracing pentagrams onto bark."

We reach a certain point in our soul-spirit journeys when we must grant a whole-body, whole-being yes to the life we are living. Of course, there may be many experimental lives along the way. We start down one road and then turn back. We encounter peculiar creatures on our path who point us in another direction. Eventually, though, we find the fire in our wills to say yes. Yes to this path. Yes to these people. Yes to this place. In that moment, we wed our souls' truth.

Imagine now that your soul is an entity that stands before you. Embodied in this entity are all your many shadows, talents, secrets, and sacred arts you are meant to unbury, polish, and show the wounded world in this particular life. This is a version of you so true, so genuine, you want to shrink from its brilliance. What do you see in this odd character, and what will you reveal to this entity now? Name what you will show this entity and begin this entry in your Book of Fire.

I met my soul, and I showed it…

In this moment, if you choose, write your wedding ritual, vows included. Here, now, you will prepare to wed your soul in ceremony. You will invite the flames to bond you to a life you choose in this incarnation.

Dearly beloved, we are gathered here to witness…
This is a ceremony of…

These fires are burning for...
In this moment, I, [chosen name], promise my soul...
I will...
I will...
I will...
These vows cannot be undone, and I choose...
I, [chosen name], take my soul to love and to cherish, in...
By the power vested in me by the Holy Wild, I now pronounce
    myself...
And so it is.

When you feel ready, set the date. May it be a solitary ceremony of initiation or one witnessed by your more magickal kin. Adorn yourself. Take to the forest, a park, the sea, or a rooftop and light a safely burning fire there. Create sacred space by acknowledging the ancestors and the directions; then read your ritual aloud with conviction.

When your ritual is finished, return to the writing and underline the important words, using these pieces to complete the second prompt that follows:

I showed my soul [what you showed your soul]
My soul showed me [your underlined words]

Fire Spell: A Heathen Desire

This is a bare-bones spell for manifesting a desire. Remember that all manifestation is also banishing. The Holy Wild exists in balance. If you choose to, for instance, cast a spell to move into a new house, you are choosing that house, that place. You are banishing all other possibilities. Before your choice, there is infinite energetic potential. After the spell is cast, that potential is distilled into that one specific thing for this one specific time. Language matters, yes, but discernment matters more.

What do you really want right now? These are uncertain times, of course. If the answer is *I'm not sure*, then the time for casting a spell is not now. Remember that the old stories say the Irish Goddess Madb or Maeve had no time for lovers who could not name three desires in a single breath.

Certainty has always been sexy. Even so, we cannot always know for sure what that next great thing is. We cannot always name what we are being invited toward. If you do know, if you feel ready, then name your proof.

How will you know the spell has worked? This is arguably not a crucial part of spell casting itself, but it is an absolutely critical component of a spell-casting practice. If you continually track your evidence that your spells work, and also, of course, note when they do not work, you will, slowly but surely, develop a Craft you have confidence in; this begins by naming your proof. If you are casting a spell for that new house, what can you say about the actual moment when you know the spell has come to fruition? Is it when you are signing the papers, moving in, turning the key for the first time, or something else? Be specific, and be sure to name the desired embodied feeling, also. If you are turning the key for the first time, are you feeling peaceful? Powerful? Safe? Wealthy? The embodied feeling is an essential part of the proof; it is how you ensure you are not moving into that new house because your old one burned to the ground unexpectedly.

Once you have named your proof, gather these simple materials: an eight- to twelve-ounce mason jar with a lid, a piece of paper, and a thing you value (an heirloom, paper money, a piece of jewelry, or something else that gives you the embodied feeling of *Yes, this holds weight; this is part treasure*).

With your materials close, begin by really envisioning the moment in time when the spell has come to fruition, when you have fully realized the *what*. Our brains always, even when we have an established Craft, will try to name the how. *How did the money come? How did I get the key? How did I get help to move?* In the container of a spell, the *how* is an obstacle. The how limits the magick's ability to support us. Outside the spell container, we still look at the listings and make the necessary moves. Outside the spell container, the how opens as many roads as possible. In the spell container, however, the *how* is constrictive and the *what* is liberating.

Cast your circle now and set the intention to stay focused on the what for the duration of the spell. If you have a circle-casting method that is in your practice, feel free to create sacred space in your own way. If these words resonate with you, feel free to use them:

To the north, to my slow-living ancestors and beloved dead, to the sacred energies of the earth, I say welcome. Bring strength to my circle.

To the east, to those old ones who spoke the language of the wind, to the sacred energies of the air, I say welcome. Bring light to my circle.

To the south, to the flame tenders and the fire dancers, to the sacred energies of the fire, I say welcome. Bring activation to my circle.

To the west, to the sea hags and the shadow walkers, to the sacred energies of the waters, I say welcome. Bring the medicine of mystery to my circle.

Hold the tension of the vision now, the proof you have named that your desire has been fulfilled, along with your desired feeling. On your piece of paper, "write it real" by describing this moment in present tense. It is already happening. Describe the moment with all your senses. You may use the prompts I offer here or create your own:

I am here, and I feel...
I am held by...
I see...
I hear...
I smell...
I taste...
I know...
I am here, and I am...

Read your writing aloud and with conviction. Begin to chant *Yes, thank you — more, please,* and fold the paper toward you. Keep chanting as you place the paper and your object of value inside the jar. Get louder and more forceful. Build the energy. If you feel called, raise the energy by chanting and moving (or drumming or singing or dancing). Raise the energy until your circle begins to feel full; then let your chant go quiet, seal the jar, sit in the fruition of your spell. Return to the vision. Feel the feeling. Stay here for at least five minutes. Open the circle by offering gratitude to the ancestors and elements from west to south to east to north. Place your hands on the ground. Breathe from low in the belly. Place your jar on your altar; then try to go outside and get some wind on your face for as long as you were in your circle. Let it be.

Fire Presences

A fire demands our presence and commands our senses. Imagine the old hooded storyteller sharing a tale around a fire. In the spaces between what is said, the flames are there. In the silence after the story ends, the fire remains.

There is an integral part of our heathen souls that speaks the language of fire, that respects the ancient role of the flame tender and knows that, like the earth and water elements, fire is life. Remember that for some of our ancestors, to let the fire go cold during the longest nights of the year meant death, and for that reason, the fire could not be ignored. Being present to the fire means providing fuel and boundaries to the flames.

Being present to the fire means discernment and containment, and our fire magick requires both. Losing the presence to fire means it might burn roughshod over the ground, swallowing all we hold dear whole, or may fizzle too soon and leave us cold. Befriend the part of you that speaks the language of the flames, that knows when to stoke the embers and when to let them be, and become the fire-keeper, the pyromancer, and prophetess.

Fire Presence I: Vows of the Fire-Keeper

"It is not a daily investment of strong will and hot rage
that is required of the fire-keeper; it is an enduring belief,
one that may burn low as often as it burns white-hot, that her
will and her magick matter. Your radical hope matters, Priestess,
and your ancestors are keeping the fire burning for you."

Witches have the long-vision. Witches understand that part of our work is to manifest a way of being in the world not only for ourselves but for the yet-to-be-born, for the children we will never meet in this incarnation. This is a volatile time to live, we know. These are the days when much is being unraveled, and there are those of us who have chosen to be here, in part, as death doula to the more tragic systems that have shaped this tired thing called modernity.

If you could light three candles now, in this moment, three candles lit in the name of three key values you wish the children born nine hundred years from now to understand, what would they be for? Name these three flames now. Show the fire what you're made of by speaking these three words aloud. Begin this entry in your Book of Fire by naming these three flames as the completion of the following prompt:

I met the flames, and I showed them…

Now write a story about a ritual the children of the yet-to-come know well, a ceremony infused with your three key values that reminds these babes why their world is so magnificent, so worthy of honor.

This is the ritual of…
It begins with the elder carrying…
Everyone who is there sees…
They bear witness then to…
They share in a moment of…
Time begins to move…
No one knows why, but…
The deep transformation comes when…
The silence tells them that…
Last, they all begin to sing…

Breathe deep. Reread your writing. Can you see it? Can you see this ceremony unfolding in your mind's eye? Imagine it into being. You've written it real, and real it is. Underline the words and phrases that feel important, and use those words to complete the second prompt:

I showed the flames [what you named the three flames from the
    first prompt]
The flames showed me [your underlined words]

Fire Presence II: The Rage That Liberates

"There is a rage that limits us and a rage that liberates us."

Some Witches run hot; their magick is fed and fueled primarily by what they know for sure does not belong in their world. They are sometimes *against* more than they are *for*, and resistance and rage are at the heart of their Craft. For these spirited ones, immense care is necessary to keep them, like a fierce fire, from burning out before their time.

A well-tended fire flows toward a slow burn; it does not require constant feeding, but it does require attention. What feels, in your world right now, as if it is on a slow burn, as if it is being alchemized not with a sudden eruption but with a careful, gradual release? Not all endings are neatly bookended. Maybe you are leaving a relationship or career, but you feel you are leaving well and with great discernment rather than due to brash and sudden decisions. Perhaps you are sensing your children growing older and the role of "parent" is shifting. You may have many life areas you could name, or you may need to consider this query for a time. When you are ready, name this long-burning fire now. What are you showing this slow burn?

I met the slow burn, and I showed it…

Grant this life area the eulogy it deserves now. Use only the prompts you feel are true for you.

In this moment, I am death midwife to…
I am loosening my grip on…
It's a slow burn, this release, but I know…
In the low light of this fire, I see…
I lay to rest my…
I honor these days of…
May you rest in peace, you…

When the writing feels finished, breathe deeply. Sense a space opening in the body. Return to the writing and underline the strong words and phrases. Complete the second prompt using these puzzle pieces:

I showed the slow burn [what you showed the slow burn from
    your first prompt]
The slow burn showed me [your underlined words]

Fire Presence III: The Original Oracle

"Fire is the original oracle."

The flames of a well-tended fire can show us much about our worlds, about the yet-to-come. Our presence is required for these visions, of course. Presence to an oracular fire borders on devotion; it does not mean merely sitting with the flames amid all the usual distractions. What would it be like to sit with a fire in solitude for hours on end without a screen in sight?

What would you wish to see in this fire, and what offering would you make to the flames in return? You would be sacrificing time you might otherwise be spending immersed in an art, a community, or another activity, yes, but could you also offer the fire your utter and complete attention for a time? How would you show the oracular flames your dedication? Begin this entry in your Book of Fire as follows:

I met the oracular blaze, and I showed it...

Before you begin the following series of prompts, spend some time with an oracular fire. This can be a lone candle burning in the dark, a massive bonfire, or any well-tended fire lit with the intention to show you what you must know. Light the fire and repeat these words aloud: *This holy moon, I see what I must see. I know what I must know. I am who I must be.*

Fix your gaze on the flames and, while you are free to move your body, try to keep your gaze on the fire. Allow the flames to be your teacher. Repeat the incantation as many times as you like, and try to be with this fire for at least an hour. Notice what you see in the flames; these visions may come as actual figures in the fire, or you may begin to see through the window of your third eye, inviting clairvoyant visions to come. When you feel ready, when the flames die out on their own or are carefully snuffed, reflect on your experience using these prompts:

I was present to the oracular flames, and I saw...
I heard...
I felt...
There were strange visions of...
I named the fire omen and witnessed...
Befriending these flames was my call to...
A fleeting thought made me wonder why...
In the ashes, I now see...

Knowing that so often a prophecy does not seem real until it comes to pass, underline any words that repeat or strong phrases, piecing together your response to the second prompt:

I showed the oracular blaze [what you showed the fire from the
    first prompt]
The oracular blaze showed me [your underlined words]

Fire Presence IV: What Lies Beneath

*"You are not your wounds; you are the fertile rich
of what lies beneath them, the primordial soul-stuff that
powers your flesh-and-bone frame."*

Along the Witch's soulful journey, wounds that were never fully healed
inevitably become reopened. Like forgiveness, healing does not mean
forgetting or condoning; it means awareness and integration. It means
bringing what lay festering in the dark into the light so it may become
more fully known, if only by you. It means integrating the woundings
into the larger story without letting the scars *become* the story.

No one makes it through this life unscathed. Sometimes there is
merit in remembering that our society is sicker than we are, that our
wounds are, in part, evidence of this; our soul is perfect, but our world
is not, and this is a painful knowing. Consider how one of your woundings in this current incarnation is a microcosm of a larger wounding
from, perhaps, the overculture to the rising counterculture. This will
not feel like a fair comparison for all woundings, of course, but see if
there is one chapter in your personal myth where you can see how it
was a larger, older story being played out in your own individual world.
Reflect on this now, using the following prompt:

I met the wound, and it showed me...

Recount the story of this particular wound now, be it a deep betrayal, a light rejection, or any hurt in between. Feel free to let your
writing become part fantasy rather than an objective reporting of what
occurred.

In the time of my innocence, I was...
I didn't recognize that beast called...
The beast came for me just the same, and I...
It's a tale as old as time, this...

Even so, my experience was mine, and I know…
My medicine was named…
The healing was like…
In my selfish moments, I wonder…
Healing can be radical when…
To my wounded younger self, I say…
To the beast, I say…
To the world, I say…

Breathe. Return to the writing. What do you notice about the emotions that came through in your words? Are there any words that repeat? Circle these. Are there any strong words or phrases that you don't quite remember choosing to write? Underline these. Use the circled and underlined words to stitch together a response to the second prompt:

The wound showed me [what the wound showed you]
I showed the wound [your circled and underlined words]

Fire Spell: Protecting the Hearth

We never wish to move the way fear would have us move, but even so, there are times in life when we must protect what we love. This is a bare-bones protection spell. To begin, gather some or all of the following materials: a writing utensil, paper, a glass jar or bottle, broken glass, bent pins, open safety pins, garlic, thorns.

When you feel ready, discern a laser-focused intention for what you want to protect. Be precise. Do not cast a spell for general "protection." Name the names, the addresses, the businesses, the creatures, and any other relevant specifics. Once you know what you want to protect, link it to an embodied feeling. Envision all you wish to protect surrounded by an egg of light. The egg is surrounded by a cube, and in the space between the cube and the egg is the "filler shield" of your choosing. It might be ice, thorny vines, fire, or a black-hole void. Source inspiration from the elements, but that space is filled by what you are naming now as the most protective substance. The outer edge of the cube is made of semipermeable black tourmaline; you push anything you like *out*, but nothing can come in unless you will it to be so. Hold the tension of this psychic shield.

With your materials close, cast a circle. You might use the following method or another that's in your practice.

Face the north. Call your loving ancestors of the north, past and future, to come closer to your circle and witness you. *To the north, to my protective ancestors, to the sacred energies of the earth, I say welcome.*

Face the east. Call your loving ancestors of the east, past and future, to come closer to your circle and witness you. *To the east, to my protective ancestors, to the sacred energies of the air, I say welcome.*

Face the south. Call your loving ancestors of the south, past and future, to come closer to your circle and witness you. *To the south, to my protective ancestors, to the sacred energies of the fire, I say welcome.*

Face the west. Call your loving ancestors of the west, past and future, to come closer to your circle and witness you. *To the west, to my protective ancestors, to the sacred energies of the waters, I say welcome.*

Touch the vision of the shield again and be sure to "see" and feel the shield around everything and everyone you are protecting. On the paper, write down all you wish to protect, and be specific. As you write, name them aloud. Get louder and more forceful. Build the energy. If you feel called, raise the energy by chanting and moving (or drumming or singing or dancing). Raise the energy until your circle begins to feel full; then let your chant go quiet. Fold the paper toward you and add it to the jar or bottle along with the other materials that will distract the negative energy should any harm come toward them. Return to the vision of the shield. Seal the jar or bottle. Feel the feeling. Stay here for at least five minutes.

Open the circle by offering gratitude to the ancestors and elements from west to south to east to north. Place your hands on the ground. Breathe from low in the belly. Bury your jar or bottle near your front door if you can. A potted plant works if you do not have ground there. And so it is.

Fire Visions

What prophecies we see in our moments of solitude, silence, and stillness show us much about who we are. No prophecy stands alone; it is channeled through *that* seer at *that* time for a reason. What do you see in the fire these days? What visions feel true in your body, like clear, clean light?

We all experience clouded vision at times. Even the greatest psychic and most skilled seer will have moments of uncertainty. In these shadowy times, we can ask the spirit of the fire to reveal only what we need to see, only what we must know. Too much information can blur our vision, but a fire lit in the dark shows only so much; it does not light and warm the whole of the world. The fire narrows the lens enough that we see only what we are meant to, and the pyromancer knows this well.

Fire Vision I: The Flames of Transformation

*"The fire element is not only a symbol of... radical hope
but also a great enactor, a driving force that moves us toward
the future we seek. All magick transforms, but fire magick purges
and activates, purifies and ignites our wills, and spurs us
onward in the face of adversity."*

Like all the other elements, like magick itself, fire is a powerful but inherently amoral force. A fire can mean life on a frigid night just as easily as it can mean death in a drought. A fire can mean warmth and light as easily as it can mean complete and utter destruction. Similarly, magick is not good or bad; it simply *is*. The hands of the shaper, the one who wields the magick and bends the energies toward their intention, determines to what end that force will be devoted.

Sometimes, it is easier to consider what we might call less baneful magick — our spells of healing and manifestation — to be somehow softer-handed than our spells of banishing; in these moments, we must consider that all manifestation is also banishing. All worlds exist in balance. If you say yes to this, you say no to that. The fire element has a ferocity to it that shows us, often literally, what profound alchemy lies in our Witchcraft.

Both fire and magick are versatile; it is the Witch who determines where they will be directed, and it is the Witch who must get out of their own way when setting this intention. The Witch who fears their own power is the Witch who stops short of invoking their most treasured dream visions. What would it feel like to name what you want, what you really, really want, without any sense of guilt? These can be desires for you, for your inner circle, or for the world at large. Whisper these wants now. Manifest them with sound. How does it feel to speak these wants aloud? Begin this entry in your Book of Fire as follows, naming your desires to complete the prompt:

I heard the sound of my desires, and they showed me…

The fires of your will are strong. Begin to consider all that would not be in your world if these desires were made manifest. Regret dampens the flames. Hesitation sucks the heat out of our magick. In choosing what you want, you are inevitably saying no to what you do not want. When we do not weave this knowing into our intention, we are unable to give the spell our devotion, the required energetic investment of a laser-focused *Yes. This. I choose this.* Describe now what will not be if your desires come to fruition.

> *I am saying no to…*
> *I hereby banish the version of my world that…*
> *I refuse to live a life where…*
> *I do not choose…*
> *I do not choose…*
> *I do not choose…*

When you feel ready, read what you have written, underline the pieces that stand out to you, weave together your response to the second prompt below; then, if you feel called, burn a copy of the writing.

> *The sound of my desires showed me* [your named desires]
> *I showed the sound of my desires* [your underlined words]

Fire Vision II: To Rise from Ashes

"Consider times in your life, my love, when you burned your world down to make space without even knowing for what purpose that space would be used and with a hawk-sighted direction that felt more belly driven than heart born. What seedlings sprouted from the still-smoking soil? What grace lay there buried in smoldering ash, and what wide-winged, mythic creature arose after the chaos cooled and the high-flamed turmoil dimmed down to warm coals?"

To see magick in all things does not mean discounting a spell cast well, the knowledge of metaphysics, or the technologies of coven Craft. There is a magick that requires great skill, and there is a magick that we are born to and with. Consider a time in your life when you cast a fiery spell of banishing, though you may not have called it such. In retrospect, you were saying no with a ferocity of will akin to what is required in a spell of banishing, but at the time, you were simply setting a boundary or refusing to accept the unacceptable. What did you show yourself in making that fateful decision?

I met myself and showed myself in that moment...

Now, if you return to that moment of decision, can you notice something new? Though this is a memory of you in that place we might call past, can you treat it like a vision and see something you had not seen before? Intentionally and with great care, can you re-member the past?

In returning to that time of..., I...
There I was becoming...
I didn't realize it before, but I see so clearly now that...
Into the fire went...
Out of the ashes rose...
With wider wings, I became a...
What wisdom there is in...

You may choose to do this same exercise with more memories where the mundane was actually magick, where you were casting a spell before you knew what a spell was. When you feel ready, return to the writing and underline what feels like valuable medicine, using these words to finish the second prompt:

I showed myself [what you showed yourself from the first prompt]
My self showed me [your underlined words]

Fire Vision III: The Weight of the Healer's Hands

"Do not succumb to apathy and stuff your healer's hands in your pockets because you were told your work was without true impact."

How heavy the healer's hands become in these times. Our healer ancestors served their small circles, their local communities, their tribes. Their role was paramount to a village and to a land. They spoke the language of the mountains and the sea. They knew every plant that grew near their homes, and they tended these medicines with great care, knowing precisely what ailments afflicted their people and what remedies the land spirits could offer. What has become of the healer in these times, when we can scroll through so many sicknesses on our small screens in a matter of moments? Just as these times warrant new stories and new ways of being, our rapidly shifting world is ravenous for radical healing.

Ask yourself in this moment what you believe the greatest sickness of our time to be. You may be able to list ailments endlessly, but for now, choose what feels like the most insidious disease. If you had a magickal object that was the precise remedy needed to cure this sickness, what would it be? Though it may feel a bit peculiar, name this object now, using its name to complete the following prompt:

I met the sickness, and it showed me…

Personal mythwork is part fantasy; it allows you to become the hero and grants your story the epic value it deserves. So easily can a healer feel overburdened by the rampant poisons surging through our psyches and our lands. It is impossible to address every crisis, and this creates an exhausting cycle of high-fire, reactive action inevitably followed by burnout and, worst of all, apathy. A personal myth keeps the story, your story, infused with a necessary meaning that speaks to your destiny, to your soul's purpose; these are weighted words, for certain, yet they are absolutely true.

The Witch has always been a healer. If you chose to claim the name Witch or healer in this life, in these times, you have chosen an arduous journey worthy of honor. You have chosen to leave the world better than what you were born to. In short, you have chosen care.

Recall your magickal object now; then write your healer's tale, using the prompts I offer or creating your own:

Once upon an apocalypse, a healer witnessed a world wounded
    by…
This healer named themselves…
The part of the world they loved most was…
In their weariest moments, they grieved for…

They struggled to understand…
In time, they learned the art of…
Only when they were ready did they happen upon a magickal
    object that could…
They learned how to wield it when…
Their greatest teacher was…
The sickness came for them just when…
In that moment, they knew…
It was never going to be easy, but…
All they had learned led them right here, to this…
The impossible suddenly became possible, and the healer began…
This was it, the…
In the end that was only the beginning, that ordinary healer had
    a magick that…
Long after the healer's bones are in the ground, the children will
    speak of the one who…

Take a long breath. When you feel ready, return to your writing and underline the words and phrases that feel important. Use this language to complete the second prompt:

I showed the sickness [your object from the first prompt]
The sickness showed me [your underlined words]

Fire Vision IV: Hearth of the Heart

"Listen, lover. I'm not interested in the ephemeral beauty of roses today, nor do I wish to hear your heady poetry. I've grown weary of oversweet romance, and I'm ready to tell you what I really want. Light a candle, lean in, and listen close. I want a love so impassioned that it ripples back through the cosmic web and stirs the hearts of the ancients. I want a love that lives on long after the flesh of these two bodies has gone cold, long after these wet lips of mine have spoken their last words and set all my secrets free. Love me like Lilith loves the untamed wilds, like a Witch loves the moon, and I promise you'll never hear a heartbeat truer than mine."

If you envision your inner altar, a sacred space just on the inside of the ribs at the base of the sternum, what do you see there? The inner altar bridges the solar-plexus chakra, the seat of our identity and sovereignty, and our heart chakra, where we affirm our ability to love and be loved. This bridge is built from a desire to be known, seen, and understood. There is a heat to our individuality, our inner fire, that warms a relationship well, and there is a cyclical rhythm to our better relationships that tempers what so easily might boil into aggression. The heart center allows us to see beauty, to find meaning in relationship to another, to a community, and to the more-than-human.

What kind of love inspires you most in your life right now? This need not be a romantic love, though it can be. Perhaps it is the love of a creature or a land that moves you in this current chapter of your life. Perhaps it is a lust others might name toxic. Perhaps it is a more diffused compassion born of an innocent awe that is beginning to mark your relationship to this wild Earth. Whatever love you name now, imagine it as an energy. What color is it? What temperature is it? What shape? What sound does it make? What do you see there inside that vibration? Name what you see to complete the following prompt:

I met a wild love, and I showed it…

Write a nontraditional love story now. This might be memoir, fantasy, or a blend of both. This is the greatest love story ever told, a wonder tale of magick and mystery.

Once, when the days were wild, an ordinary Witch went out in search of…
Early in their journey, they saw an omen that spoke of…
What they didn't see was a misty spirit that was the very embodiment of the love that…
The spirit followed them, met them in their dreams, and…
They didn't know it, but what they were searching for was also searching for them, and soon…
One cold night when the ghosts were loud, the Witch met…
It was fate, for certain, and…
By the time the sun rose, the misty spirit had taken its throne upon the inner altar of that Witch, and…
The happily-ever-after was really a…
The real blessing was always…

Return to the writing when you are ready and underline the stronger words. Use these to create your response to the second prompt:

I showed this wild love [what you showed this wild love from the first prompt]
This wild love showed me [your underlined words]

❧ *Fire Spell: The Spiral of Self* ❧

The manifestation of our desires often requires a shift in belief, an internal transformation to better accommodate the external transformation. This is not a simple process, particularly for deep and long-held belief systems that are socially supported; these beliefs do not go quietly into that good night. These beliefs do not want to die, so we must prove to ourselves they are untrue and outmoded. For instance, we can cast an abundance spell, but if we do not believe we deserve this abundance, the spell will inevitably fail to fruit. Of course, the casting of the spell itself causes necessary changes, but those changes are unlikely to be permanent unless the old belief systems can be dug from the psychic soil, roots and all.

Consider the spiral of the self, the understanding that the external landscape of our lives reflects, in part, the internal landscape of our psyches. Name a life area that feels stuck right now. Importantly, know that stuckness is not always negative and is sometimes a necessary part of the conversation you are having with a new creative project or way of being in the world. But, for this spell, name a life area that feels stuck and you are ready to see start moving. Once you have chosen the life area, select a stone that represents this life area to you somehow.

Ask yourself what the desired outcome is. How will you know you have become unstuck? See yourself in a yet-to-come moment in time when you are feeling the complete fruition of the spell; something has given way, and you are living the desired outcome. Can you see it? Ask yourself now: *What new belief does this version of me have that I do not yet have?* Also ask, *What old belief has this version of me shed that I still hold?* You may need some time to get clear on these two beliefs, the one that must go to make room for the one that comes and the one that resources your desire. Imagine that the new belief is the bridge between you in the present moment and the version of you in the yet-to-come who has seen the stuck become unstuck.

When you feel ready, create sacred space by acknowledging the four directions, your ancestors, and the elements. Bring the stone you selected with you, along with a writing utensil, piece of paper, burn bowl, and fire source. Write down the old belief on the piece of paper, loosely fold it away from you nine times, set it aflame, and watch the fire burn. As the smoke rises, sense the old belief being shaken loose and uprooted. Feel some space being made in your body.

Then take hold of the stone and begin to chant the new belief with conviction, naming it as absolutely, infallibly true. Keep chanting until you feel a subtle change in the stone, in you, and in the space around you. When it feels finished for now, open your circle and place your stone on your altar. Ask yourself now: *What proof do I need that this new belief is true?* Name your evidence. How can you prove yourself right?

Make a list of five or more possible ways you could be proved correct. For instance, if the new belief is *I have the right to feel safe in my home*, then you might name evidence such as *I am eating alone and slowly, comfortable in my kitchen, and breathing easily*. If the new belief is *I have the right to be paid for my art*, then your proof might come when someone pays you for your work. Importantly, do not name evidence you know is impossible for you to gather. In the latter example, if you have no art for sale, you are unlikely to receive proof your new belief is true. Keep the roads open for your evidence to be received, and allow unforeseen proof to find you as well. In other words, your proof might come in ways you have not named in your list.

For the next nine days, you will be on watch for your evidence that your new belief is true. At the end of each day, you will go to your altar where your stone rests, and you will think of a moment from that day when your new belief was proved correct. Hold the tension of that proof and add "energetic deposits" of smaller stones, shells, seeds, or coins that are slowly spiraling around the central stone in this order:

Day 1: Recall a time today when your new belief was proved correct. Repeat your new belief, and add one energetic deposit next to your central stone.

Day 2: Recall a time today when your new belief was proved correct. Repeat your new belief, and add one energetic deposit next to your central stone.

Day 3: Recall a time today when your new belief was proved correct. Repeat your new belief, and add two energetic deposits next to your central stone, beginning to form a spiral around the belief stone.

Day 4: Recall a time today when your new belief was proved correct. Repeat your new belief, and add three energetic deposits.

Day 5: Recall a time today when your new belief was proved correct. Repeat your new belief, and add five energetic deposits.

Day 6: Recall a time today when your new belief was proved correct. Repeat your new belief, and add eight energetic deposits.

Day 7: Recall a time today when your new belief was proved correct. Repeat your new belief, and add thirteen energetic deposits.

Day 8: Recall a time today when your new belief was proved correct. Repeat your new belief, and add twenty-one energetic deposits.

Day 9: Recall a time today when your new belief was proved correct. Repeat your new belief, and add thirty-four energetic deposits, completing the Fibonacci spiral around the central stone.

Leave your altar up for at least three days after you have added the last of your energetic deposits. Notice how you feel when you are met with the proof that your new belief is true, and notice if these moments feel more frequent now. And so it is.

Testament to Fire

The third "testament" will be your Testament to Fire. Begin by writing an invocation to the fire element. You may use the prompts I offer here or create your own:

This is my testament of flame, bone fires, and ash. I am setting to burn all...
I am asking unanswerable questions of...
To the fire, I say...

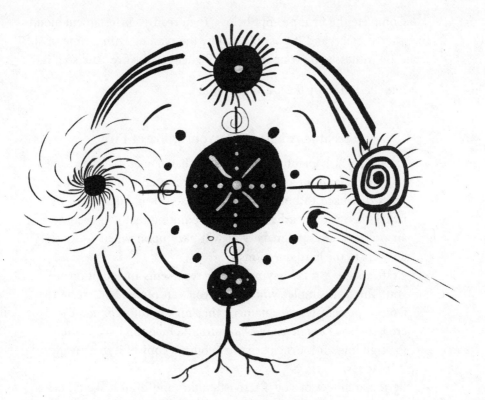

Go back through your Fire Reflections, Presences, and Visions, and look to the last line from all twelve journal entries. Stitch these together to become your "Fire Verses":

Verse 1: The fire showed me…
Verse 2: Fate showed me…
Verse 3: Rage showed me…
Verse 4: My soul showed me…
Verse 5: The flames showed me…
Verse 6: The slow burn showed me…
Verse 7: The oracular blaze showed me…
Verse 8: The wound showed me…
Verse 9: The sound of my desires showed me…
Verse 10: My self showed me…
Verse 11: The sickness showed me…
Verse 12: This wild love showed me…

Complete the final prompt below. Then read your testament aloud in a sacred place, and if possible, follow the reading with a time of silence. Be witnessed by your ancestors. Be held by the fire. And so it is.

I am here, held by the fire, and I know...

Possible Additions to Your Book of Fire

- Create an "ash painting." Consider what names you used to claim but claim no longer, the beliefs you used to call true, the vows that used to bind you. Write these down, burn them in ritual, then use the ashes to create a painting that will become an oracle, a strange image you will gaze upon when seeking answers to the hard questions.
- Craft a sigil, a sacred symbol, that represents invigoration to you. This is a simple symbol that you can remember, created from a present-tense statement that makes you feel empowered, such as *I am here, and I am strong*. Once you have written the sigil in your journal, be sure to burn a copy of it to activate its potency.
- Be the architect of your "activist's altar" and draft a sketch of what this altar might look like. What symbols speak to you of your core values and deepest currencies? What would remind you to press on when the world gets rough? Let this altar be a touchstone for your activist's will, a remedy for apathy, and a reminder that you have permission to rest as needed. Plan it, build it, and tend it well.

Book Four

The Book of
AIR

Heathen Verses of the Griever's Breath

*T*he air element speaks the language of balance and trust. Every breath is a gift we receive and offer in return. Our air is the precise blend of elements we and the Earth's flora and fauna require to live, yet this miracle cannot readily be seen. We trust that the air will always be present, will always be the right recipe for us to survive.

Our air magick is subtler than that of the earth, water, and fire. Our relationship to air is less tangible, more difficult to discern, yet we trust it is there. We are full of a heathen faith in this invisible nourishment, and the kinship we feel with the air has much to teach us about ghosts, deities, ancestors, and other spirits that might resource us, though we cannot see them with our human eyes.

When you write your Book of Air, begin to let the unseen Others speak through you. Sense the thick energies surrounding you and the thinness of the veils between all worlds. Hold a sense of trust in the Otherworld as you write the words that want to be written, that can be written only by your hand.

Word-Spell: Songs of Breath and the Wild Hunt

The harvest moon was fading behind the peach lace curtain of dawn, and she, that hooded ghost of a once-arrogant woman, bade me sink back into sleep a little longer. The sun would wait, she promised, but the wild hunt would not. I obliged without protest, letting her pull me under the indigo dream sea of my more wicked and oracular visions, and she wrapped her ice-blue finger bones around my wrists, hummed a throaty tune of foolish carnage and love lost, and hauled me straight to the bottom.

In those all-too-familiar haunted depths, I readied myself for prophecy. I vowed to befriend my monsters, and the ghost Witch kept up her mournful song while I built a circle of humble cairns out of shell and stone in the name of dead lovers, soft-breasted but bitter-hearted grandmothers, and the many wounded women I used to be. When I finished my work, the song fell to silence, and I was alone in my sanctuary of shadow with only my will and the dull thrumming of my aging heart to keep me warm.

I knelt at the center of my fragile grief monuments and squinted into the dark, whisper-praying verses of dying hope and intentional awe; all the while, my pulse beat swelled and quickened in an ancient rhythm only the most peculiar Pagans, outlaw ocean currents, and oldest trees remember. The flesh was drummed away from my bones. The niceties were cleansed from my tongue, and my blood spilled into a spectral cloud that danced and twirled without skin to contain it.

I heard it then, a fury of horse hooves beating in time with my own wild heart, and I stood to meet them the way they should be met, these omens of looming doom. I knew all my foremothers knew in that moment that the wild hunt was riding, with my death-masked rebel ancestors leading the way, that an old dream was exhaling its final breath, and my for-once-unprotected heart called these undead warriors right here to see their bone-daughter in all her rawest glory and grief.

They rode 'round my hand-built graveyard, encircling my shrines in their frenzied swirl while they howled and hissed, dragging a crumbling crystal-bone Earth behind them in the dust. A soft song in a language I do not speak rattled from my throat and spilled from my lipless mouth, and I opened my arms to receive the anguished carcass of a fallow planet. The hunters stilled themselves and joined me in my keening, and I wailed from the depths of my most primal soul while the riders rolled the beloved rock of the world into the center of my bone grounds.

Their black-as-night horses stomped in time, meeting the drums of the wild ones and calling my own heart to pound so madly I feared what was left of me might crumble to dust, but our song kept on. The mud-and-gray marble once called Home quivered between us, and this band of heathens was joined by the wild flame-tending children who had yet to learn apathy. I knew then we were singing green and loamy flesh back to the bones of a dying Gaia, and the ancient dead joined the loving descendants in this eleventh-hour ritual to reanimate a world slaughtered without honor, an elder mother pierced between the shoulder blades by her most ungrateful creatures and left to bleed out in the dirt.

We sang as grief ritual and apology, as offering and eulogy. The resonance was so potent that a spirit erupted from the sound, a winged entity born from the womb of ceremony that was the very soul of our song, and we all knelt in the name of good death. Even the horses took to the ground, and we prostrated ourselves before the once-virile mother who bore us.

Live, live, live, live, live, we chanted into the ground, and our tears fed the empty soil.

Live, live, live, live, live, I whisper-wept, and the song's spirit wrapped its wings around the Earth.

I woke with the words still rolling from overdry lips, skin blue as juniper berries and eyes streaked red with the memory of it all. I breathed a soft homage to the wild hunt, to the children, and to the ghost Witch who wanted me to see such ritual; then I went down to the sea to pray.

To Begin Your Book of Air: An Artful Invocation

Begin your Book of Air by tuning in to the rhythm of your heart. See yourself now beating out this same rhythm on an ancient drum, standing high atop a cliff overlooking the sea. Be windswept here. What song does this vision sing to you? This is a soul song. This is a hymn of the heart. If you hold the tension of this vision, how do you feel? Begin to draw intuitively now. Create an image that sings the same song, and let the image reveal something to you, something you had not realized before this very moment.

Allow each of the following questions to then spark another image, symbol, or word. Surround your soul-song image with your strange answers to these questions. Take as much time as you require to honor this, the moment your Book of Air was born; then move through each of the twelve journal entries at your own pace, in your own time.

> When did you feel a whole-heart longing for someone, something, or someplace?
> What does longing, love, grief, and gratitude feel like in your body?
> What does it mean to receive well?
> If you tune in to the desires of the heart now, what are you being invited toward?
> How are you the gift?

Story Lantern: The Blood Cloak

Read this story spell aloud if you feel called. Let it be a guiding lantern illuminating precisely what you need to know now, today, as you read these words. Add any images the story sparks or words from the story that feel potent to your artful invocation that begins your Book of Air.

Some say the gods left the air long ago, but I say the air is god. I, the blood-hooded Priestess, say we are still here. Sing for us.

Wherever you are, whoever you are, sing. Sing wild lullabies of quickening seeds, frozen mud, and those mythic mountain dwellers who speak the language of wolves, who live as sacred and snow-loving poets, who still

tend their cave altars for the lovers, the makers, and the innocents, even and especially now. Sing for them.

May the seas not reach them, these hooded-with-shadow folk who glow with an earthen belonging we humans have yet to know. May the moon howl their low stellar anthems with a silver-light resonance so potent the Witches and the storytellers hear it as they daydream, and may their bones be marked green with the sigils of these slow-living heathens, these Pagans before there were Pagans.

I'm loudmouthed today, you know. I'm honey-tongued and ready. Let me tell you of my cloak of blood.

Long ago, when the land was full of ghosts, I longed to tend an altar in a temple of stone. So great was my longing, every breath that slipped through my lips was thick with want. My blood was heavy with my desire, and I let the rivers of me stain my cloak when the moon was new. I let the righteous rivers run from my womb and onto the cloth. I sang over it then, this garment made of me, and, I tell you this, that cloak began to breathe.

I made a cloak so holy that it was a living woven entity. When I wore my red cloak made of breath and blood, the winds would howl, the storms would come, and I became a Priestess of the air, a Witch of the wind. I became an elder dreaming the wounded world whole again by firelight, listening to the west wind with a silent drummer's patience. I walked into the wind, and I set my mind to building my temple.

Some say the gods left the air long ago, but I say the air is god. I, the blood-hooded Priestess, say we are still here. Sing for us.

I raised my hood and met the king on the road. I stood in his path with palms raised and eyes open. I demanded the land for my temple be gifted to me, and he laughed in my direction.

Still, I did not move. I stood there in that road, and I took my hood down. I asked again, and again that king refused.

The winter winds began to howl, and I unwrapped the cloak from my body. I told the king he would give me the land my cloak would cover, and he conceded, seeing only with his short-vision.

I cried out then. I cried out to the winds of the north, to the hearth holders and the devout wolf mothers. The wolves came from the woods and pressed their bloody paws into the snow, stamped the ruddy print on the sacred cloth, and sang a new vow northward just as the winter sun split into one hundred million golden rhymes, just as this cosmic poetry surged through the wilds like heathen honey. The wolves took the cloak in their jaws and stretched it to the north for as far as that king could see.

"Only what my cloak will cover," I said.

I cried out again. I cried out to the winds of the east, to the wild makers and rebel artists. The aching artists with pain in their hearts and holiness in their hands walked out of the dawn and pressed their clay-coated palms onto the sacred cloth. They, these heathen makers, these blessed freaks, scream-sang a new vow to the east just as the seeds split through their shells, just as an unnamed masterpiece was formed from ice, blood, and well water, just as the last of the frozen rot melted into gold-green loam. The artists took the cloak in their hands and stretched it east for as far as that king could see.

"Only what my cloak will cover," I said.

I cried out once more, this time to the winds of the south, to the hooded warrioresses and flame tenders whose names I will never know, and the naked fire dancers walked out of the storm and beat their drums until their hands ached. They pressed their feet into ash and printed the sacred cloth with the heat of their dance, hissing a new vow to the rain just as the full moon became a god, just as the spirit of the moment marked us all with venom and bone broth, just as the wild children took to the streets, carrying the edge of my cloak into the south as far as the king could see.

"Only what my cloak will cover," I said.

Again, one last time, I cried out, this time to the winds of the west, to the keening women and the wounded healers. They walked out of the gloaming wailing in the name of truth, and those Priestesses hummed a somber dirge for the simplicity of winter. The willows wept over the frozen well, and the dead stirred in their depths. The mourners let their tears fall on the sacred cloth and wept a new vow to the west just as the late-winter sun turned pink, just as the blind raven shed a feather for the old way, just as a bolder sky crowned a quieter world. The healers took my cloak in their hands and carried the edge into the west, as far as that arrogant king could see.

"Only what my cloak will cover," I said, and he admitted his folly and gifted me what was due. I built that temple of stone to stand just as it did in my dreams, and I forever blessed my blood cloak for carrying all the magick I needed, for housing the heat of my desire and the wisdom of my voice.

I hung my cloak on a spring sunbeam inside my hallowed temple, and I spoke bold words to those who would join me here:

> May this cloak of medicinal blood and sacred flame reach the edges of this forbidden place. May we dance long and howl moonward, and may we remember why we came here to this time and place. Only what our cloaks will cover.

Guiding Story Remembrances

Feel free to answer any or all of these queries in symbols rather than words, finishing your artful invocation that begins your Book of Air.

1. When have you been the blood-hooded Priestess facing the king on the road?
2. What parts of the story, if any, feel like timely lessons for you?
3. What does the symbol of the blood cloak mean to you now, in this moment? What does your cloak cover?
4. What else did this story lantern illuminate for you?

Opening Spell: A Storm of Infinite Potential

This simple practice might be a spell on its own, or it may be a useful supplement to any manifestation spell. Begin by naming a clear vision that longs for you, a fleeting moment in time that you want to live, that you can begin to feel into with all your senses. Where are you? Who are you with? What tastes do you have on your tongue? Be here in this yet-to-come moment with all that you are.

Begin now to describe aloud one potential road for how you arrived at this particular moment in time. Be creative and dream new possibilities. Try to name at least one influence on your path between now and this future moment you have never thought of before.

Get even weirder. Name another potential road here. What's the strangest possibility you can envision for how you arrived here, to this vision that longs for you? Describe this new possibility out loud, letting it be even more bizarre than your first described journey.

Give it one more go now. Sense the expansion of possibilities. Name an even more peculiar, more serendipitous road that led to this vision.

This is not a practice of limitation. You are not deciding exactly how your vision will come to fruition, but you are allowing yourself to dream stranger possibilities. Name every miracle you can think of that might lead you here. Dance while you do it.

As you write your Book of Air, let this sensation of infinite possibility guide you. Let the more restrictive patterns be broken and leave room for the wild unseen to resource you in the most unexpected ways. And so it is.

Air Reflections

In moving from earth to water to fire to air, our magick becomes less tangible. We have more questions than answers. Our intentions become less concrete, and we welcome a fertile befuddlement. Our guiding stories are of love, grief, and the infinite, those alchemical tales of union and dissolution, of nurturing Goddesses and lost queens. Reflecting on the presence of the air element in our memories invites us to consider the heart in all its intelligence and experience. Consider your story in relationship to all other stories. Become larger than your own single thread in this grand green-blue tapestry called Earth.

The air bids us to see the subtle vibrations that surround us, to scry our prophecies from smoke, and to allow all binaries to crumble. We welcome new imaginations here, and we sense the eternal flow of the breath beyond what we might call the inhale and the exhale. We ask now, what is left when the fire cools? What remains after the last of the smoke has cleared, and what never-before-seen mythic creature will rise from these ashes?

Air Reflection I: To Die and Begin Again

"The Witch of Sacred Love is an openhearted lover
who embraces vulnerability with outstretched arms,
who has witnessed the ever-turning wheel of waxing, fruition,
waning, and void. Despite all heartbreaks and hardships,
this Witch knows all must die so all may begin again."

When we speak of our vulnerability within the context of relationships, we speak of our tender places, the soft and raw parts of ourselves where we could be seen so easily. There are times in our lives when vulnerability is a considered choice, when we decide to let ourselves be known by another; in these moments, we feel exposed and unprotected. We allow our heart-walls to be breached in the name of intimacy, and we learn what we are truly made of in these times of courageous connection.

We have a level of vulnerability we are comfortable reaching, and we have a boundary we do not move beyond; this boundary was set during childhood and fortified every time we were rejected, abandoned, or betrayed by one who claimed to love us. In time, in relationship, we are not only the ones who maintain that wall; we *become* that wall, so much so that to soften this boundary feels like a death.

Reflect now on a moment when you chose to allow someone to step beyond the wall and your worst fears were *not* confirmed. Your old pattern was not reinforced, and a long-held belief about safe limits in relationship was, in essence, proved false. What part of you died in that moment? What did you witness in the story of your own becoming? Begin this entry in your Book of Air by naming what you witnessed.

I told my story, and I witnessed it…

Our world can be sharp, we know. When we get cut enough in our younger years, we become incredibly skilled at avoiding any place, anyone, that could hurt us. We decide what is safe. We create our own rules, and we make our world smaller than it needs to be, in the name of self-protection. For this reason, it is essential we take stock of the moments when our expectations were proved wrong, when the friend who seemed too sweet to be real was incredibly supportive or the hooded stranger offered us directions in the dark. We must collect our proof that people are empathic creatures, that humanity is worth saving. We are offered such evidence every day, but our patterns allow us to ignore this proof too easily.

Tell a rare story now. Tell a tale of vulnerable moments when there was no great wounding that followed, when strange helpers along the roadside told you where to go and odd healer creatures gave you exactly the medicine you needed.

> *In the time of my innocence, my heart-wall was built from…*
> *Strong and steady it stayed until…*
> *One peculiar day, I met someone who showed me the meaning*
>   *of…*
> *I couldn't believe it, but they were…*
> *Though much happened in between, there was another soul who*
>   *allowed me to…*
> *I was wary, but they were…*
> *In the time of my wisdom, my heart-wall was built from…*

Return to the writing and underline the sections that feel like an elixir for the hardened heart; use these words to complete the second prompt:

> *I witnessed my story* [what you witnessed from the first prompt]
> *My story witnessed me* [your underlined words]

Air Reflection II: The Healer's Road

"The healer's road is long and unpaved, and part of our task is to strike a balance between directing social evolution and surrendering

> *to the parts of the healing process that are organic and already*
> *occurring in their own way, independent of our actions."*

Not everyone claims the name healer, but many are doing the sacred and arduous work of healing themselves, even when they do not show it, post it, or name it. A skilled healer understands that only so much of the process can be shaped, because the medicine has an intelligence of its own. The medicine understands where it must go, and the healer is not in complete control of its journey. A surrender is required, then, by both the healer and one being healed, and surrender is, as we know, never easy in a society that values power and certainty.

What have you witnessed in your own healing journey that felt like a necessary letting go, a loosened grip, or retracted claws?

I felt my healing, and I witnessed it…

If all healing is awareness and integration, much of this lifelong process is about pulling what we would swear was not ours out of the dark and cradling it, naming it, and giving it a home. Such is the work of the shadow walker.

Your shadow is the deepest part of you, hidden so long it has become cold, monstrous, and hungry for lack of love. This will not be easy, but tell a tale now about who you are not, about all you would swear you could never be, about the vilest monster who has ever walked the Earth.

The long-fanged creature who would wreak havoc on these lands
> *was called…*
The creature believed…
The creature fed on…
The creature's weakness was…
Cities rose and fell while this beast ravaged…
No one remembers how it happened, but one day the monster met…
With words of welcome and love, the monster softened into…
In the end, the villain became the…

Return to the writing and underline the words that particularly repulse you. Weave them together to finish the second prompt:

I witnessed my healing [what you witnessed from the first prompt]
My healing witnessed me [your underlined words]

Air Reflection III: The Ancient Antidote

"Hail and welcome, she who is feared for her wise ways
and hand-brewed ancient antidotes to the particular poison
that is relentless and uncontained power hunger."

Not so long ago, there was a strategic, successful church-led and government-sanctioned war on healers. We call this the Witch-hunts and the burning times. These were the dark days that continue to haunt, continue to play out in other forms, laws, and institutions. In many ways, the burning times continue, and this knowing can limit the ways the Witch works in the world. What have you witnessed in your life that continues to silence you or restrict the medicine you have to offer? This is an experience from childhood when you were told to discount what might become your unique healer's genius, your most sacred work in the world. What did you witness in that moment?

I tasted the poison, and I witnessed it…

Now, be brave and reinvent, re-member, this moment. If it feels right, reshape the moment so that you become the remedy to the disease that would seek to destroy your healer's power. Revision. Reimagine.

Once upon a childhood, I knew…
That day, what I wanted more than anything was to…
I was told that…
They wanted me to be silent, but instead I became…
They wanted me to become invisible, but instead I became…
You'll never believe it, but I was an ordinary child who carried
the medicine of…
Even today, they tell the story of the brave babe who…

Imagine the entire scene, including you and all the players who were there in that moment, being surrounded and filled with a diamond-bright light. Breathe from your belly and hum slow and low as you exhale. When you feel ready, return to the writing and underline the words and phrases that feel potent; use these to shape your response to the second prompt:

> I *witnessed the poison* [what you witnessed from the first prompt]
> *The poison witnessed me* [your underlined words]

Air Reflection IV: Becoming the Wolf-Woman

"One day, I may come to know a wise Wolf-Woman who hand-built her own stone cottage on a mountaintop, where she speaks to the ghosts of burned women, smokes homegrown mugwort, and waits for young women thirsty for truth to come and sit by her hearth. One day, she might teach me the most moving benedictions to unnamed deities while I sip nettle tea and knit blankets for her horned billy goats, and, just maybe, she will write a primal prayer just for me. Until then, this is the truest prayer I know."

Our childhood wishes about what the world would become, about who we would become within that brighter, bigger world where all things were possible, can feel as if they've fallen short in these days of rising seas, burning forests, and enormous human-versus-human conflicts. The myths that fail to fruit are a source of grief, indeed, but answer this: If the child version of you could see who you have grown to be, what would they be dazzled by? What would this innocent who you used to be love to witness about your life and your world?

> I *met the child, and they witnessed me…*

Write a letter to them now. Tell them about your life and world, about whom you have met and what you have learned. Tell them of the wonders of simplicity, the many enchantments of the natural world.

> *Dear Innocent, please call me…*
> *I will call you…*
> *This is going to be hard to understand, but I am you, a bit older and a lot…*

I've been in love with...
My favorite part of the day is...
Once, I met a wise medicine keeper who...
I'm really amazing at...
I've learned to...
I see beauty in...
I still do what you love to do and...
One thing I must say is...
Always remember...
I love you, and...

Breathe. Return to the writing. When you feel ready, gather your puzzle pieces by underlining the words and phrases that feel special; then use these to create the response to the second prompt:

The child witnessed me [what you witnessed from the first prompt]
I witnessed the child [your underlined words]

❧ *Air Spell: Portals of the Haunted Heart* ❧

Our hearts are mansions full of our ghosts, named and unnamed. There are rooms we rarely visit, haunted by relationships that ended without closure, words left unsaid, deaths left ungrieved. Sometimes it is a struggle to be fully present in a new relationship when we are still haunted by our old ghosts; a part of us stays caged in the past wondering what might have been, expecting old patterns to resurface, or relying on outmoded boundaries that have long since crumbled.

This is a spell of space clearing, an exorcism of the grass-is-always-greener demon, and it will not be for everyone at all times. This is a spell of sovereignty, of choosing the road you are on. If you feel ready, begin to imagine your psychic home, your House of Becoming. Begin in your "Room of Comfort" and imagine this first room in your house as a true sanctuary; everything here in your Room of Comfort makes you feel safe. Time moves slowly here. Imagine moving through your Room of Comfort and seeing all that lives there. If you see anything that does not belong, let it go. Gift it to the ether, to the void, and trust that it is gone.

When you feel ready, leave your Room of Comfort and imagine entering the "Inner Sanctum" in your psychic home. This is a large space from which innumerable hallways, staircases, and other passageways branch off. This is the holiest of holies. How does this space look to you? How do you feel when you are here? This is a psychic space of infinite possibilities.

Find now your "Room of Relationship." Notice how the portal to this space looks. Is there a symbol on the door? Is there no door at all? Look without judgment, but discount nothing. When you are ready, set the intention to enter your Room of Relationship and move through a psychic space clearing. Move into the space with conviction. See here the ghosts who haunt your heart. Say to them what you never said. If it feels right, ask them to leave you. Tell them to go. If you meet a ghost you do not necessarily want to banish but also do not want to remain a resident of the heart, direct them to your "Room of Grateful Memory"; this is their new home now. Watch them leave.

Move through your Room of Relationship and clear the haunted spaces, one by one. Feel the frequency rise, and with every ghost that goes, notice how the colors become more vibrant here. What songs do you begin to hear the clearer the room becomes?

If it feels right, shape this room as you wish it to be shaped now. Do you want there to be an altar of beauty with candles eternally burning? Make it so. Do you want to create a space for someone new to join you here? If so, how do you want this space to look? Make it so. Tend this space well. Let it be an imagined reflection of your exquisite and extraordinary heart. Let its rhythm be the rhythm of your pulse beat, and let it show you something you did not realize before now, before the room was clear.

When you feel ready, knowing you can return here as needed, leave your Room of Relationship and return to the Inner Sanctum and, last, to the Room of Comfort. Take a few breaths here in this sanctuary space, offer yourself gratitude for doing this work, and, finally, return to the tangible world. Ground yourself here. And so it is.

Air Presences

How can we be present to what we cannot see? We are always being invited to witness the invisible, to be in relationship with the stories of the heart that live only in memory. We cannot see grief, love, forgiveness, or empathy, yet we trust in their existence. The air element prompts us to be present to the many rhythms of the heart, that hidden intelligence that bridges the gap between self and other.

A practiced discipline is required when we become present to the unseen. We are wired to see what threatens us first and to leave the subtle visions for when we feel safe and secure. Similarly, it is difficult to tend to the health of the heart when we fear abandonment or betrayal, when our sense of relational safety is imbalanced. To be present to the air element means to consciously build trust between the human and the beyond-human, to foster an intimacy between certainty and mystery.

Air Presence I: The Breath of the Sacred

"Ours is a land of soulful diversity,
and the depth of human experience negates the
possibility for universal norms and static beliefs."

One of the many cracks in the foundations of organized religion is the assumption that we must all believe in the same gods, the same stories, and the same moralities. No two people will experience divinity in precisely the same way, and to be present to the air element is to acknowledge the cyclical nature of our unique spiritual experience. The sacred, like our breath and our love, is both given and received in a personal rhythm. There is both balance and flow to our conversations with the Mystery, with whatever we conceive God to be, and there is no one-size-suits-all prayer, song, or holy book for everyone.

Take a moment now to bear witness to your own unique spiritual journey. See it in your mind's eye as if the whole of the story were a map, with your many teachers and temples, desperate prayers and ecstatic celebrations, all laid out before you. Witness the journey now from its inception to the current chapter. What do you see?

I took the journey, and I witnessed it...

Invite the present chapter to reveal itself to you now. If your spiritual journey were an epic novel, when do you feel the current chapter you are living began? Do you feel you are midway through this part of the tale? Is it only beginning or drawing to a close? Let this chapter be a story of cycles, of deep connection to the sacred, diving into darkness, and coming back again. When you feel ready, title this chapter:

The Story of...

Write parts of this chapter now, using the prompts I offer here or creating your own:

It all began with a knowing, a knowing that...
I was so certain that the...
The certainty did not last, though, and so soon I felt darkness come toward...
I fumbled for a time, struggling to see...
Again, then, the dawn came, and I understood...
I saw...
I became...
I knew for sure what my new name would be, and it was...
In time, even this new name transformed into...
I softened, yet again, and released...
Into shadow I went and...
I knew then that holiness meant...
I know now that initiation means...
I am...
I am...
I am...

These are uncertain times, indeed. Sometimes we find the only truths we need from our own stories, our own patterns. When you feel ready, return to the writing and find the exact medicine you need there. Underline the words and phrases that stand out, reorder them, and create your response to the second prompt:

I witnessed the journey [what you witnessed about your journey from the first prompt]
The journey witnessed me [your underlined words]

Air Presence II: An Elder Earth

*"In our collective evolution, how can we now be the
community we needed when we were younger...?"*

Even in our direst moments, we can allow ourselves to be held by two
key truths: we grow to become the teacher we needed when we were
younger, and it serves us to live as though we are a microcosm of the
world we wish to see. Perhaps our human community is in its adoles-
cence. Perhaps we are just beginning to allow our systems to mature into
their strongest forms, to release our more selfish tendencies in favor of a
more global individuation. If so, then how can we dream — how can we
all dream — of a yet-to-come human society that will best parent this
one, in its most volatile and metamorphic state?

What does an elder Earth look like when it remembers its adoles-
cence? What has an elder Earth remembered from the time of its innocence that modernity has chosen to conveniently forget? What leaves an
elder Earth awestruck at its own beauty?

I saw the elder Earth, and I witnessed it...

Consider your own story now and how much you have grown from
the time of your youth. No two stories are the same, of course, but we
can all mine our own lessons from the depths of our personal myths.
Imagine yourself as parent to a younger version of yourself, just as the
spirit of the elder Earth is a nurturing source of support to our dis-
jointed civilization. Hold the tension of this knowing, and write freely
in response to the following prompts:

In the time of my youth, I was...
In the time of its youth, modern society is...
My weakness was...
If modernity has a fatal flaw, it's...
In the time of my wisdom, I have become...
*When the human community emerges from this cocoon, it shall
      be...*
Said the elder Earth to the children, "Always be..."
Said the elder Earth to its younger self, "Welcome to..."

Strange musings, these are. When you feel ready, return to the writing and underline the potent knowings; use these to create your response to the second prompt:

> *I witnessed the elder Earth* [what you witnessed from the first prompt]
> *The elder Earth witnessed me* [your underlined words]

Air Presence III: The Circle's Soul

"This is what binds the circle together. This is the power source that holds the potential not only to infuse the intentions of each member but to feed the shared vision for a juster humanity that undergirds this particular communion. If the circle is an entity, then this vibration is its electric pulse, its pranic flow, its very life force."

There are times in life when we might wish to work with a group of magickally minded individuals — when our own solitary practice seems not to nourish us in the way we wish to be fed — yet, for varied reasons, we cannot circle with our coven. Perhaps we have yet to find our people, or perhaps distance separates us from our most beloved Witch kin. In these times, it serves us to remember that we are not and have never been alone. If we stand in solitude in our living rooms and raise our hands in the name of a better world or a better life, we have tens of thousands of years of ancestors standing with us. We are always held by the wild unseen, and our separateness is an illusion.

Can you see yourself now? Surrounded by those beloved dead who know you best? Take a moment and see if you can sense their presence, these grandmothers whose names you will never know, these older-than-ancient spirits who speak through you, who carry all the medicine you need in their long memory, and these yet-to-be-born star-children who see you as their primal ancestor. Feel yourself held by them, your own story carefully woven into the grand quilt of your ancestral story, which is a lone circle in the global tapestry, itself a lone circle in the wild intergalactic fabric.

I saw the ancestral circle, and I witnessed it...

Let your breath's rhythm ground you in this moment. When you feel ready, imagine one of your most loving ancestors stepping forward and whispering through you. Imagine their will animating your hands as you write this, their channeled wisdom, their poetic elixir brewed just for you at this peculiar time in your life:

> *These days, these times in the Earth's story, are indeed…*
> *I was with you when…*
> *I am with you when…*
> *I will be with you when…*
> *The ancestors have seen such things before, and we can tell you…*
> *Breathe deep and know…*
> *Look to the setting sun and understand…*
> *Tonight, may you dream of…*
> *May you wake with a new knowing that…*

Take a moment and offer gratitude to the ancestors for speaking through you. They are here, and you are here, held together by the strong strands of deep time. When you feel ready, return to the writing and mark what feel like essential words right now; use these to complete the second prompt:

> *I witnessed the ancestral circle* [what you witnessed from the first prompt]
> *The ancestral circle witnessed me* [your underlined words]

Air Presence IV: Dear Innocent

"Oh, dearest innocent! I see you now, resting your damp forehead on your scarred and shaking knees. May you weep all you like, for no one can rob you of your right to feel, not tonight when the ghosts of lost souls have risen to encircle you with the truest, warmest spectral grace, not tonight when your tears are holy water blessing the fertile ground from which a better humanity will bloom."

To be innocent does not mean to be naive. To be innocent means to hold the wild tension of awe even and especially now. Times are dire, yes, but all our strategic planning and rational, educated thinking has gotten us here, to the brink of climatic and societal collapse. What solutions might we be invited toward if we saw our problems through more innocent eyes? We do not need to choose innocence over knowledge necessarily; we need only to allow innocence to temper our certainty. What we need now are new ways of thinking about old struggles, and to see through more childlike eyes is to see hope in the midst of hopelessness, possibility shining like gold in the muck of impossibility.

Imagine "innocence" as an objective energy now. Feel no need to bind it to any memory or experience yet. Just imagine what the spirit of innocence looks like. What color is it? How big is it? What sound does innocence make? Describe this energy now and begin this entry in your Book of Air.

I met innocence, and I witnessed it...

From your own life now, choose an area of transition you might call a problem. For your first experience of this work, it is best to not choose what you might rate the greatest problem in your life right now or the sharpest source of stress. Choose an area of focus that feels pressing but not so much so that it consumes your thoughts. Invite the spirit of innocence to step into your body, to beam through your mind's eye. As you move through the following prompts, try to consider this problem from an entirely new perspective; this is easier said than done, of course, but for each prompt, set the intention to think of just one new glimmer of insight regarding the issue:

> *There is not just this or that; there is also...*
> *A miracle might step in and suddenly show me that...*
> *I never thought about it quite like this, but maybe, just maybe...*
> *Now, I have to wonder if...*
> *There are helpers I have not yet named, and they are...*
> *I see now that...*
> *What a wonder it is to...*
> *The solution, I think, will be sourced from...*
> *Through more innocent eyes, I see this newfound way of...*

Take a breath and notice how you feel in this moment, having transcended at least a few tried-and-true thought patterns you could have easily fallen into. Did you use words you have not used in a long while? Return to the writing and see what you find. Underline what feels like the most telling phrase, and use it to complete the second prompt:

I witnessed innocence [what you witnessed from the first prompt]
Innocence witnessed me [your underlined phrase]

Air Spell: Love Thyself

Our relationship to self is a microcosm of our intimate relationships to others. By extension, our relationships to others are microcosms of our relationships to community, to the world at large, and to the divine. Tending to our relationship to self is, then, a vital act of nourishing all other relationships.

If every relationship is a conversation of the heart, then what are you saying in your kinship with self? What could be better said or made clearer? How can you nurture yourself *now* in a way that would make the elder you proud?

Prepare a ritual bath for yourself now and allow every ingredient to represent something you would like to honor about yourself, about who you are becoming. An essential oil of lavender might represent your right to rest; mint leaves might represent your strong voice. Imagine the elder you preparing this bath for the present you. As you add the ingredients, change the conversation you are having with yourself; make it more honest, compassionate, and nourishing. Speak aloud words to yourself you have not said before.

Let this be a healing bath initiating you into a new relationship with yourself. Channel the yet-to-come voice of the wiser Witch you are becoming. As you prepare the bath, parent the present moment.

When you feel ready, breathe deeply, inhaling the scent of the bath. Hold the breath as you step into the water with intention. Exhale, sinking into the warmth, and know that you are leaving your old way of relating to yourself behind. You are setting new patterns. You are cleansing yourself of dusty doubts and the muck of self-loathing. You are letting the water wash away the soil of what was, the masks of shame and the too-tight tethers of childhood. Do not take this spell lightly. This water is a well of wisdom brewed by the elder you. Bathe well. Hold the tension of the moment. Let this be a ceremony so epic that a spirit arises from the water, an entity born of your becoming. When you feel ready, rise from the water reborn. And so it is.

Air Visions

The heart has eyes of its own. The heart sees what fear does not, the possibilities that exist beyond the boundaries that no longer make sense, past the fences we erected during our younger years to keep us safe from what we called forbidden. Now, into the wilds we go, reclaiming innocence once more and testing both the integrity and necessity of our many protective walls.

Relationships are entities. Like small gods, they require nourishment to survive. They require prayers of loving action, altars built from conversations full of truth, and devotional songs of empathic understanding. Relationships want their stories told and told well. They have their own poetry, their own language. Any relationship is an energetic container through which meaning is sought and made, shaped by those in conversation with one another, and our visions of what is possible in a relationship expand this container, create a larger vessel for growth and evolution.

Air Vision I: The Alchemy of Relationship

"The magick of the air element is that of connection, the alchemy of relationship, and the beauty of all our many intimacies."

When we see solutions through more innocent eyes, we are seeing the third road, the hidden passageway between the binaries. The very nature of our language reinforces our this-or-that thinking. We are socialized to think in opposites — truth or lies, right or left, male or female — but our world is a spectrum of intricate possibilities and fertile complexities. Our stronger relationships prove how we are always in conversation with the infinite. We are always arriving at the third road when we listen to one another empathically, when we compromise and collaborate. A sound relationship is a new entity born of separate individuals with a shared intention, and a relationship can house limitless potential.

Consider one of your strongest relationships now. This might be a friendship that has endured against all odds, a nontraditional partnership, a traditional marriage, or a circle of more than two people. This might be a relationship that has ended or one that continues living. Now, regardless of where the relationship is in its lifespan, consider the energy of the relationship itself. How was or is the relationship an entity, and how was or is this spirit fed and nurtured? Describe this entity now to begin this entry in your Book of Air:

I found a relationship, and I witnessed it...

Tell the story of this relationship now as if it is its own character, with its own personality, desires, and distastes. What might you name this relationship spirit, and how might you describe its journey?

Once upon a time, there was a spirit called...
The spirit was born to wild hearts who...
The spirit was at its most vibrant when...
The light of the spirit grew dimmer in those moments of...
The spirit loved...
The spirit detested...
The greatest test to the spirit's strength came when...
Even then, the spirit knew...
Over time, the spirit grew to be...
These days, the spirit still...
To this spirit, I say lastly...

Offer gratitude to this spirit if it feels right. When you are ready, reread your writing and mark the important words and phrases, the language that feels like a teacher, and use these words to finish the second prompt:

I witnessed a relationship [what you witnessed from the first prompt]
A relationship witnessed me [your underlined words]

Air Vision II: Like Honey Wine from the Magdalene's Tongue

"I am the Witch of Sacred Love, and I was born into this body to
share what wisdom I can, to feel my feelings fully and own the
majesty that is me. I am here and I am staying, and what I have
learned from my many woundings and healings will drip from my
lips like honey wine from the Magdalene's tongue."

We are born to be in conversation with our ancestors and descendants, with what we might call the past and the future. While we owe no one our story, we know that parts of our personal myth can serve the collective. Aspects of our lived experience are integral to the larger whole. Consider now if there is a chapter in your healing journey you have kept secret but now feel ready to share, an experience you have learned from and sense might benefit others in turn. Share just a small piece of this now, completing this prompt to begin this entry in your Book of Air:

I felt my transformation, and I witnessed it…

If you feel ready to, write about this experience now, this soul-designed healing that made you wise, knowing that you need not share this writing with anyone.

Sometimes in life, there is before this and after this. For me, there
*   is before… and after…*
Before it happened, I was…
After it happened, I was…
I don't want to tell you how…
If I'm being honest, the wisdom came only when…
I might call this wisdom I have to offer the…
To the young ones who have not yet seen what I have seen, I say…
To the old ones who have seen what I have seen, I say…
Healing is…
Healing is not…
Wisdom is…
Wisdom is not…
I wonder now if…

If it feels true to your practice in this moment, read what you have written aloud, if only in a whisper. Allow yourself to be witnessed by the unseen Others. Notice the most potent phrases as you read, underline them, then use these to complete the second prompt:

I witnessed my transformation [what you witnessed from the first prompt]
My transformation witnessed me [your underlined words]

Air Vision III: The Ministry of Unanswerable Questions

"In moving from air to ether, we become less tangible and less sure. We question what we know about the death-life-death cycle, divinity, and all the psychic mysteries that, for all our nature walks and communal sharing, remain unsolved."

We live in a time of generative befuddlement, of fertile confusion. Surely the butterfly must be perplexed when it dissolves into a puddle of imaginal cells; the creature is driven toward its inevitable metamorphosis nonetheless. What in your life right now feels as if it is dissolving, perhaps of its own volition? What feels as if it is falling into oblivion? Witness this now.

I met my metamorphosis, and I witnessed it...

Ask the unanswerable questions now. Let the tension of confusion be the womb of potential. Hold the discomfort of not knowing and do not try to answer your questions and make them statements. Simply let them be. Let them remain questions. Let them become teacher. Learn from them.

I have an unanswerable question in my heart about the future, and it's this:
I have an unanswerable question in my heart about death, and it's this:
I have an unanswerable question in my heart about magick, and it's this:

I have an unanswerable question in my heart about healing, and
    it's this:
I have an unanswerable question in my heart about divinity, and
    it's this:
I have an unanswerable question in my heart about children, and
    it's this:
I have an unanswerable question in my heart about my art, and
    it's this:
I have an unanswerable question in my heart about vision, and
    it's this:

Still allowing the questions to remain questions, when you feel ready, return to the writing and underline the strong words and phrases, using these to complete the second prompt:

I witnessed my metamorphosis [what you witnessed from the
    first prompt]
My metamorphosis witnessed me [your underlined words]

Air Vision IV: A Joyous Death

"In lieu of flowers, please send joy and jazz. Forget the
somber blubbering, sickening scent of overpriced wreaths,
and white pearls on black dresses. Forget the eulogies and verses
mumbled by someone I did not know to a God I didn't believe in. ...
Give me a death ritual where the brightest colors are worn
by the dreamers and the poets, for no one is a mourner
at the memorial for the wildest life I have ever lived."

In preparation for having a child, a parent might be encouraged to create a "birth plan," complete with who should be in the room, what music should be played during labor, and all the contingencies and variables should something unexpected occur. Why, then, are we not as encouraged to have death plans? Unlike giving birth, we know for certain we will all, someday, experience death.

How do you wish to be remembered? What stories do you wish to have told at your funeral, and what is your vision for your death ritual? Be witness to this now, and begin this entry in your Book of Air as follows:

I saw my death ritual, and I witnessed it...

Now write a eulogy worthy of you. Become a seer poet and speak of who you were, though you still *are*. Befriending death is the greatest shadow work we can do, and much of our modern poisons are derived from our collective fear of death and darkness. Name death now for what it is: absolutely inevitable and a portal into the unknown. Death is not the end, we know. Nature shows us this truth every day. Death is an initiation, a rite of passage we will all take.

Dearly beloved, we are gathered here to celebrate the dancing spirit of...
In life, they were known for their...
In death, may they continue to be known for their...
May we anoint their grave with...
Let us sing now. Let us sing the song called...
Let us drum and dance in joy, for this holy wild soul was surely...
What they will miss most about life is...
What they will love most about death is...
Can you see them now, smiling for...
To them, we say...
May they rest in joy and...

Feel the rhythm of your heart-drum. Feel your breath. You are alive. You are here. When you feel ready, reread what you have written and underline the pieces that feel like medicine; use these to complete the second prompt:

I witnessed my death ritual [what you witnessed from the first prompt]
My death ritual witnessed me [your underlined words]

❧ *Air Spell: Drumming the Heart* ❧

Life has a rhythm we seldom hear, and it is the rhythm of our heart-drums. This is a simple and small spell of tuning in to the rhythm of our creaturely selves. When you feel ready, face the direction that feels like home. If you have a drum, allow this sacred instrument to resource you in this ritual. You might also use your two hands on your thighs or the ground. You are welcome to sit or stand.

Begin by placing a single hand on your heart. Feel the rhythm of your pulse and begin to chant in time with your heart: *I am, I am, I am, I am, I am.* Once you are immersed in the rhythm, begin to drum in time with the chant, your chant of the heart.

Invite your drummer ancestors to come a little closer to you, to dance slow in time with your song. You may be met with mystical visions here if you stay long enough. You may find yourself suddenly suspended in time. Invite your ancestors to keep you grounded, to show you what you must see.

Stay here for at least twenty minutes if you can. When you feel ready, let the drum go silent first. Return a hand to your heart and feel the rhythm. Let the chant go quiet then and simply be here. *I am, I am, I am.*

You are, you are, you are.

And so it is.

Testament to Air

The fourth "testament" will be your Testament to Air. Begin by writing an invocation to the air element. You may use the prompts I offer here or create your own:

> *This is my testament of wind, smoke, and breath. I am hearing the breeze through the trees, and it whispers…*
> *I am asking unanswerable questions of…*
> *To the air, I say…*

Go back through your Air Reflections, Presences, and Visions, and look to the last line from all twelve journal entries. Stitch these together to become your "Air Verses":

Verse 1: I witnessed my story…
Verse 2: I witnessed my healing…
Verse 3: I witnessed the poison…
Verse 4: I witnessed the child…
Verse 5: I witnessed the journey…
Verse 6: I witnessed the elder Earth…
Verse 7: I witnessed the ancestral circle…
Verse 8: I witnessed innocence…
Verse 9: I witnessed a relationship…
Verse 10: I witnessed my transformation…
Verse 11: I witnessed my metamorphosis…
Verse 12: I witnessed my death ritual…

Complete the final prompt below. Then read your Testament to Air aloud in a sacred place, and if possible, follow the reading with a time of silence. Be witnessed by your ancestors. Be held by the four winds. And so it is.

I am here, held by the air, and I know…

Possible Additions to Your Book of Air

- Write a love letter to yourself in ten years. Let it be part devotion, part prophecy, and part manifestation. Seal it in an envelope, and write on the outside, "Open on..." followed by the date of exactly ten years from the day you write it.
- Create a sacred smoke recipe for blessing your home. Let every ingredient represent something you wish to see fill your home. Perhaps juniper represents otherworldly connection and lavender represents embodied peace.
- Write a poem that reveals a secret about you that you are not ready to share with anyone. Let it be cryptic. Only you understand its meaning. Only you can choose if and when you are ready to reveal this secret.

Book Five

The Book of
ETHER

Heathen Verses from the Unseen Others

*E*ther is the space between. In tales of initiation, there is always the death, the severance that bids us leave the ordinary behind, but this death is never immediately followed by a new birth. What follows the death is the void, the liminal space, the 'twixt and 'tween.

Time moves differently here in this void space. We have no pattern for the hours, no clock or calendar that makes sense. We are outside of what we know, and we have no vision of what may come. Tending to this moment of gestation through our sheer and fiercest presence is the greatest gift we can offer that future version of ourselves, the one who has made it through, who has been reborn.

Let your Book of Ether be your strangest one yet. Look to the tales of the hag, the Yagas and the Cailleachs. Use words you have never used before. Write words of paradox and mystery. Say anything that has so far been left unsaid in this, the last book in your *Holy Wild Grimoire*.

Word-Spell: Songs of the Cauldron Keeper

Deep in the cosmic caverns called the World's Womb, a lone cauldron keeper stirs her brew. She midwifes the birth of innocent galaxies on the edge of the universe and whispers blessings for a long life. She licks the prima materia from her spoon and stirs on, driving the dance of the older than ancient, humming soft songs into her bottomless pot of what is and has always been.

She feels every death. Every eruption of a failed star quakes inside her bones. Every earthly creature curling under a tree to become rot has a home inside her heart. Every interplanetary collision and argument between the gods is a rattle in her throat, and every fallen tree is an ache in her belly. Even so, she stirs on. She never stops. She stirs the world awake and asleep, to life and to death.

To Begin Your Book of Ether: An Artful Invocation

Begin your Book of Ether by drawing an image that speaks the language of the stars. Let visions of galaxies spiral-dancing and ravenous black holes be your muse. Sense the great expanse and infinite wonder of space. How does it feel to be an earthling who belongs to this one blue-green rock orbiting a mighty round fire? Reflect the numinous on the page.

Allow each of the following questions to then spark more imagery, symbols, or words. Fill your page and feel no need to offer concrete answers. Solve nothing. Take a moment to honor this, the birth of the spirit of your Book of Ether; then move through each of the twelve journal entries at your own pace, in your own time.

Who are your gods?
What are your childhood memories of the moon, the sun, or
    the stars?
What would a celebration of your life after your death look like?
What ghosts still haunt you?
What prophecies do you hold for the world?
What does it mean to be a seer in these times?

Story Lantern: Return of the Mist Dwellers

Read this story spell aloud if you feel called. Let it be a guiding lantern illuminating precisely what you need to know now, today, as you read these words. Add any images the story sparks or words from the story that feel potent to your artful invocation that begins your Book of Ether.

Some say the gods left these ethers long ago, but I say the ethers are god. I, the mist dweller, say we are still here. Sing for us.

You might not see me, but you know me. Surely you have felt my breath on your neck and heard my voice in the fog. You are this hag's child. You are my kith and kin. Crawl into the hollow of my belly and let me tell you of my people.

We dwell within the mound and mist. We live inside the lightning. We are the children of the green-skinned grandmother called Danu, and we are alive, well, and waiting.

Long ago, before the land, sky, and sea were ravaged by men, we lived as you live. Our songs were different, but the weight of our bones and our flesh was much the same as yours. When the folly of the human quest became too great, we slipped away into the mist. We became weather. We fell into the wind, and there we stayed.

We stay there still, even now. We stay, and we wait. We wait for the sea to speak wild. We wait for the fields to rebloom, and we wait for that human animal to remember its true name. Until then, find us in the fog.

Find us where you might not wish to look. Find us and wonder if we, the mist dwellers, are a once-and-future echo of you. Find us and wonder if we are humanity remembering itself whole. Whisper into the dark ethers of evening and bid us return.

Some say the gods left these ethers long ago, but I say the ethers are god. I, the mist dweller, say we are still here. Sing for us.

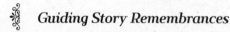

Guiding Story Remembrances

Feel free to answer any or all of these queries in symbols rather than words, finishing your artful invocation that begins your Book of Ether.

1. What parts of this small story spell speak the loudest to you now?
2. What can you say about the hidden parts of our world, about ghosts, angels, and that field of unseen intelligence that seems to hold us?
3. What else did this story lantern illuminate for you?

Opening Spell: The Misty Bridge

This is more a strange imagining than a spell. Allow this brief practice to resource you in times of pressing uncertainty, to illuminate only what must be seen. If you have a particular life area you would like clarity on in this moment, begin by asking an unanswerable question about this life area.

Imagine you stand on a misty bridge suspended over softly running water. The fog is so thick, you cannot see farther than your hand can stretch. You are here, yet you feel safe. You feel swaddled in the blankets of the unknown. You feel held by the hidden wisdom field that somehow organizes your story, that you can sense only when you step back from the day-to-day rhythms and see the whole of your life's song. Begin to breathe deeply now, and with every in breath, imagine you are inhaling this mist, drinking in the essence of the mystery. As you exhale, you breathe out a diamond-bright light. Inhale mist; exhale light. Stay with this until a new knowing arises, until you see a symbol, an image, a being on the other end of the bridge.

What do you see there when the mists clear? Know that what you see may not make immediate sense. Even so, take note. As you write your Book of Ether, hold the tension of this mythic image you witnessed when the fog lifted. Name it teacher. And so it is.

Ether Reflections

Our memories of the ether are our ghost stories, those moments we have all had when the Otherworld came back for us, the times in our lives when what we sensed was real did not match what we were told could be real. To reflect on the ether is to take stock of our strangest encounters, to honor the shadow times, and to offer gratitude to those invisible ones who held us in our moments of void when the wounds were loud but the loving ancestors were louder.

Ether is space. Even less tangible and more ubiquitous than the air element, the ether surrounds you even now. Look at the spaces around you and find the quiet energies there. Remember the moments when you thought you were alone but were reminded otherwise. A Witch knows the ether element well, for it is here that the conversation of a spell takes place. It is here the Witch does their work, in the spaces between what is absolute.

Ether Reflection I: The Space Between

"Ether is the space between, the realm of spirit, and the void.
Here, in this fertile darkness that spans the liminality between
death of the old and birth of the new, we rest in perfect grace.
We are neither creating nor releasing, neither manifesting
nor banishing, neither planting nor harvesting."

To befriend the ether, the space between, is a radical act. We are social-ized to be constantly expanding and consuming, yet we all yearn for rest.

Consider the times in your life when you entered into a void be-tween this and that; something had ended, but the new *something* had yet to begin. Perhaps you had moved from a home but had yet to root in another place. Perhaps a relationship had died, but another had yet to be born. Choose one of these past voids, a memory that feels alive for you now, and ask yourself to recall a fleeting moment within that particular void. Can you see yourself in that moment, staring longingly into the autumn sunset from the window, weeping on the cold kitchen floor, or quietly praying into the fire? Sift through your memories and find a snapshot in time that is of you consumed by the fertile dark void within which a new life, a new way of being, had yet to begin. How were you marked in that moment? Begin this entry in your Book of Ether by describing how the void marked you.

I saw the void, and it marked me...

Take a brief inventory of your void memories, pulling these uncom-fortable moments from your mind like oracle cards. What are the first ten void memories that seem to bubble to the surface from its depths? Make a list of these now, only describing them in as much detail as you require to reference the memory later. Now ask yourself whether you see any patterns in these void memories. Is it often winter or nighttime? Are you often alone or with others? Is there music playing in many of your moments? Discount nothing. All patterns are relevant even if they seem inconsequential. Tell what seems to be the common story of your void now, drawing from whatever patterns you have found in your in-between times.

I was in between. What had ended was...
What had not yet begun was...
The void that swaddled me felt like...
There, in the ether, I wondered why...
Time was...
Time was not...
I was haunted there by the ghost named...

In the worst moments, I wept for...
In my best moments, I hoped for...
Now, in the time of my wisdom, I understand...

Having considered a few of your many voids, ask yourself now what your greatest void medicine might be. How would you have liked to be held or nourished there in the cosmic dark? Can you create a plan to manage the next void when it comes, a strategy of ritual, rest, and reflection?

When you feel ready, return to your writing and underline the words that feel potent and strange; use these to complete the second prompt:

> *The void marked me* [how the void marked you from the first prompt]
> *I marked the void* [your underlined words]

Ether Reflection II: The Greatest Challenge

"We face our most significant human challenge in this fertile void; we ask ourselves why we are here and how we came to be. We sift through our experiences, our stories, our wins and losses, hoping to gift our existence with a meaning beyond the roles we have played in our lives."

The unique journey we are meant to take on this wild planet is soul-designed and shaped largely by what we do not know, by the truths we long for and the mysteries we alone are meant to solve. If we knew all there was to know about ourselves, the gods, and that trickster vixen we call the future, we would not encounter the creatures we are meant to meet. We would not experience the joy and the grief, the pleasure and the pain, we are meant to experience in order to create the art we were born to create.

The void is the fertile womb from which our soul-designed life emerges again and again, initiation after initiation. There is a reason why people turn to divinity in times of great loss; sometimes we require the fallow times in order to see how spiritually rich we are. Sometimes we need the space left behind when some great thing falls to bones so that we may see more clearly, with vision uncluttered and hearts broken wide open.

Can you reflect on a time in your life when you were in your depths but came to a new understanding of the meaning of the sacred, God/Goddess/Goddex, or whatever name you prefer for the cosmic infinite? This is a time when something had fallen away and what arose in the space left behind was a newfound belief or understanding about why we are here and how we came to be. How did this new knowing mark you during those rough times?

I met the sacred, and it marked me...

You might return to the list of void memories from the previous Ether Reflection exercise or create a new one, but this time, rather than searching for the void patterns, search for the epiphanies, the lessons that emerged from these shadows, the sudden knowings that, if you stitch them together, become a true tapestry of brilliance showing you how far you have come, how wise you are, and how truly wondrous your story is. Recount these from-out-of-the-void lessons now:

Once, I was taught that...
In a moment of anguish, I realized...
This is not a story of defeat; it's a tale of...
My homecoming happened when...
I suddenly knew why...
The shadow times gifted me with...
I never told anyone, but I learned a secret when...
A subtle voice told me that...
It was darker than dark, but I could see...

Our greatest knowings do not come from academic settings; they come from *void school*. They come from our own depths. Return to your writing and underline the important pieces, the jewels of understanding that have been recovered from the numinous dark. Use these to complete the second prompt:

The sacred marked me [how the sacred marked you from the
    first prompt]
I marked the sacred [your underlined words]

Ether Reflection III: The Witch's Psychic Soil

"Deeply embedded fears of the dark, death, and divination
consume meaningful space within the Witch's psychic soil.
There are those of us who are chosen to be Death Priestesses, feeling
at home in the ethereal space between death and birth, finding
comfort in ghostly communion, and living a little more in the
shadows than those drawn to more brightly lit corners."

Much of modernity's power, the grip of the overculture, is maintained by our societal aversion to death, grief, and aging. The Witch has always held hands with the dark, and the burning times were driven largely by a strategic church- and state-sanctioned goal of ridding the world of those who understood the merit and inevitability of death. The healers, the Pagans, those who lived close to the cycles of the land — they understood too well that death is a natural part of life, and this knowing did not serve the governing agenda.

To sense a kinship with death and darkness is to live better, to craft a lifescape full of meaning and joy, and this does not serve capitalism's need to keep us unfulfilled and in a constant work-for-more and strive-to-be-better state of being. To be heathen is to live on uncultivated land, and to live on uncultivated land is to know that death is a portal we all are destined to walk through. As we move into the next age, when all our binaries, including life and death, begin to give way to a greater spectrum of wisdoms, there are many of us coming into a renewed relationship with death and dying.

Consider the first time you met death as a child, perhaps with the loss of a beloved pet or a loved one leaving this world for the next. If you witness yourself in that moment, what do you see?

I met death, and it marked me...

Consider this now: if you were to leave the flesh house you've been living in since you were born in this current incarnation, what would you miss the most about our pleasure planet?

Were I to die today, the face I'd miss the most is...
The taste I'd long for is...
What I'd miss most about autumn evenings is...

What I'd miss most about winter midnights is...
What I'd miss most about spring mornings is...
What I'd miss most about summer days is...
I'd miss the smell of...
I'd miss the songs of...
Today, I'm alive, and I will meet this moment with joy, with...

Read through your writing. Drink it up. Can you glean a small ceremony from your writing, some intentional, simple ritual you might do today to feed your flesh? Underline the words and phrases that feel important, and complete the second prompt with that language:

Death marked me [how death marked you from the first prompt]
I marked death [your underlined words]

Ether Reflection IV: The End of the Hunt

"No more do your threats of hellfire and damnation scare me. This little girl is all grown up, and I stopped following your dress code years ago. Find me here. Find me there. Find me everywhere you don't want me to be, if you will. I'm not running anymore. No more, for the hunt has ended."

The Witch wound runs deep. It's a scar on the wild feminine soul. It's the monster in the corner disguised as a holy man. It's the nagging voice that wonders what will happen if the neighbors see, and it's the inner beast who wants to keep you safe and small, protected by invisibility. There are many childhood wars we still fight though they have long since ended. There are battles the still-in-shadow parts of our psyche are waging even now, and the Witch knows well that these inner conflicts are echoes of the burning times.

Consider now how the Witch wound has marked your story, your lineages, and your sacred work in the world. There may be fear, rage, grief, and rebellion. There may be spiritual oppression, betrayal, shame, guilt, or rejection. These are all sharp words. Find your own language now to describe the indescribable:

I met the Witch wound, and it marked me...

Just as the Witch requires proof that their magick works, that their spells are effective and omens are real, the Witch needs regular proof that the hunt has ended. We know, of course, that the hunt does continue in subtler forms, within institutions that seek to control bodies and minds, within the laws that seek to govern what cannot be governed, within systemic racism and environmental degradation. In all these ways, the hunt continues and the burning times rage on. How, then, can we declare the end of the hunt? How can we feel liberated in our own work when the atrocities continue?

The collective trauma of the Witch-hunts is too great for any one Witch to take on; to do so would freeze our magick. What we can do is consider our own story and our own liberation. We can consider how we ourselves have healed and how our particular story is a continuation of our grandmothers' healing. In what ways are you safe in your Witchcraft? Recall moments now when you saw magick in the world, in your life, and no one came for you. Harvest memories when your Witchcraft was medicine and not poison, the very healing salve you needed for the wound that still bleeds.

> *I knew for certain magick was real when…*
> *A Witch is…*
> *A Witch is not…*
> *In a rare moment of revelation, I let them see me…*
> *No hunter came for me when…*
> *I still keep secrets, but I understand…*
> *Secrets are…*
> *Secrets are not…*
> *My Witchcraft is a remedy for…*
> *My Witchcraft is an art that…*
> *More than this, my Witchcraft is the reason why…*

To discern when to work in the shadows and when to work in the light of day is a challenge for the modern Witch. There are secrets we still must keep hidden. There is magick that is more effective when it is not visible to all, but this does not mean we hide because we are afraid. Consider now when you hide because of your power and when you hide because of your fear. Sense the difference in your body between secrets sourced from boundaries and sovereignty and secrets sourced from fear.

When you feel ready, return to your writing and underline the potent words and phrases, using them to complete the second prompt:

The Witch wound marked me [how the Witch wound marked
    you from the first prompt]
I marked the Witch wound [your underlined words]

Ether Spell: Removing the Seer's Obstacles

Even the greatest seer finds their vision clouded at times. This is a simple spell for embodied obstacle removal. You will need a piece of paper, a writing utensil, a "thing of no value" or something you are ready to throw away that somehow represents the obstacle to your vision, clearing herbs such as juniper or cedar, a burn bowl, a fire source, and something that represents your "clear sight," your strong vision.

With your materials close, cast a circle. You might use the following method or another that's in your practice.

Face the north. Call your loving ancestors of the north, past and future, to come closer to your circle and witness you. *To the north, to my seer ancestors, to the sacred energies of the earth, I say welcome.*

Face the east. Call your loving ancestors of the east, past and future, to come closer to your circle and witness you. *To the east, to my seer ancestors, to the sacred energies of the air, I say welcome.*

Face the south. Call your loving ancestors of the south, past and future, to come closer to your circle and witness you. *To the south, to my seer ancestors, to the sacred energies of the fire, I say welcome.*

Face the west. Call your loving ancestors of the west, past and future, to come closer to your circle and witness you. *To the west, to my seer ancestors, to the sacred energies of the waters, I say welcome.*

Name the obstacles you are releasing now as best you can. Perhaps they are a fear of "seeing too much too soon" and a belief that your "visions are not real." Ask yourself where this thing is in your body. What color is it? What temperature is it? On your piece of paper, "write it gone" by telling the obstacle to go. Use all the ferocity you've got. Why does it no longer belong? Why does it hold no power over you? You may use the prompts I offer here or create your own:

You are nothing to me, and I am free of you because…
To you, I say…
You are already gone from my world, and I feel…

Read your writing aloud and with conviction. Begin to chant *No, be-gone, away with you,* and fold the paper away from you. Keep chanting. Get louder and more forceful. Build the energy. When you feel ready, burn the paper and begin to move in ways that break up the energy of the obstacle in the body. Go for ten to fifteen minutes if you can. Chant and move. Watch the smoke rise. Your clue that the energy-raising phase is ending will be a subtle (or sometimes not-so-subtle) energetic shift in the body. Move until you feel the change.

Let your chant go quiet while the ashes cool. Feel the new feeling. Stay here for at least five minutes. Cover the "thing of no value" in some of the ashes once they have cooled. Open the circle by offering grati-tude to the ancestors and elements from west to south to east to north. Place your hands on the ground. Breathe from low in the belly. To end the spell, carry the thing of no value to the trash and release it. If it can be buried ethically, without poisoning the ground, you might do so in a place you don't regularly visit. Dispose of the remaining ashes, and do not look back. Let it be. Place your object that represents your clear vision on your altar. Tend it well. And so it is.

Ether Presences

To be present to the ether is a constant practice of walking with one foot in each world. The Witch cannot be entirely in the realm of the heavy, the material, and the known, nor can the Witch live completely in the ether. Healthy presence to the ether element is shaped by the Witch's dance between the seen and the unseen, between the universal stories many would understand and the magickal stories reserved only for those who speak the ethereal language.

Ether Presence I: To Live on the Fringes

"The heathen, the Witch, and the wild woman have always existed on those socially unacceptable edges, and, in the ether, we stand arm in arm with the freaks and the outcasts. We will ourselves forward in

the name of what we know is true, and we expand
the boundaries of what we once thought unreachable."

The trickster archetype lives on the outskirts of the overculture. They are an edge dweller, dancing on the fringes of the center and having no desire for celebrity. In some ways, the Witch is a trickster. The Witch prefers the freedom of the fringes to the spotlight of the center, and for that reason, the Witch will always keep parts of their life from being known and seen.

For the Witch, there is a tension between the desire to shape societal changes and the need to stay hidden. In the wonder stories and the fairy tales, the Witch in the woods is to be feared. She will eat your children and poison your crops. You will go to her seeking healing, but she'll curse you instead. We know these tales were used to convey the atrocious social conventions of the times, with solitary women deemed outcasts and, by extension, targets. We know this, yet there remains a lure to the introverted wild-woman archetype. In dire times like these, the longing to escape the dominant culture is palpable and fierce, but the edge dweller does not seek escape; the edge dweller seeks mobility.

For certain, there are areas of our lives where we feel the desire to stay just on the edge. We let some aspects of ourselves be seen and known and keep others shrouded in shadows; when this is intentional and considered, there is a wild power about such secrecy. When this is passive or reactionary, the opposite is true and we allow the monsters in the dark to control us.

Ask yourself which areas of your life presently feel as if they exist quite intentionally on the edges of what is acceptable. These are parts of your world that you prefer be seen just enough — by you, by your people, and by your community — but not in their entirety. They are seen and they are not seen, as if there is a single beam of light that hits just one aspect of this life area, though the deep magick may lie in the shadows. What does it feel like to keep this part of you both visible and invisible at the same time? There is power in paradox, after all, and we so often believe all secrets to be weakness; this is not so. Some secrets are absolutely necessary, absolutely integral to our authenticity. What about you is both seen and not seen? What part of you dwells on the edge? Begin this entry in your Book of Ether as follows:

I met the edge, and it marked me…

Tell the edge dweller's story now. Let it be as fantastical as you want it to be. Hold the mystery that comes from writing about a paradox, a tension that, by nature, transcends language.

I was born to live on the fringes of a society that…
I built my house on the boundary between…
There, I dance to a rhythm that confounds the…
I move to the center from time to time. I let myself be seen just
*   enough to…*
I always let them see my…
I sometimes let them see my…
I never let them see my…
I return to the fringes when I feel…
To dwell on the edge means…
Here, with my fellow freaks and holy heathens, I am…

Know that the nature of our edge dwelling is always changing, and we need this to be so. The Witch is always bringing what was previously shunned toward the center, then returning to the shadows. Our borders expand. Our secrets get strategically exposed. We want this to happen so we can keep digging in the dark. Such is the story of change; such is the role of the Witch in these times.

Return to your writing when you are ready and underline the medicinal words and phrases, using them to create your response to the second prompt:

The edge marked me [how the edge marked you from the first
*   prompt]*
I marked the edge [your underlined words]

Ether Presence II: Sovereign within the Collective

"I am both sovereign and at one with all that is. Hear my joyful heartbeat, Mystery; it's drumming out an ancient anthem just for you."

A key knowing that often gets lost in the wilds of neo-Paganism is that the Witch is and has always been both sovereign and a part of the collective; this is why Witchcraft is political. How can it not be, given history? The overemphasis on individuality in Witchcraft is unfortunate, particularly if we are taking our lessons from nature. Our solitary magick works when we are in conversation with the *all*. We are not separate from or superior to the energies with which we work, and, importantly, there is both power and surrender in this understanding.

Find an object now in your space that you feel reflects your current state of being back to you. This can be anything, though natural objects like stones, flowers, or shells lend themselves to this practice well. Set a timer for five minutes, fix your gaze on your object, and ask it to teach you something, to help you remember something about your world you may have forgotten. You may move your body or make sounds, but keep your gaze fixed on your newfound teacher. You will begin to notice that your inner narrator — the voice in your head that is constantly describing your experience, telling you when it is too hot or wondering if you remembered to feed the cat — gets quite loud during this practice. Let it. Let the inner narrator speak, but keep your gaze fixed. You then might notice that your eyes begin the "optical illusion" stage of this exercise and you start to see your object go fuzzy around the edges, levitate, multiply into three, and exhibit any number of other strange visual effects. Let this happen, too. Keep your gaze fixed.

It takes practice, but what you will begin to notice is that when the inner narrator has said all it can say and the optical illusions have been befriended, something new and unnameable arises. There is a softening of everything — the object's name, color, and shape along with your own name and roles and all other ways you identify yourself. There is an immense magick to this moment, a true connection to the ether, when you become sovereign within the collective. You are this object, and this object is you.

Once you have finished this experiment, complete the following prompt:

I saw the ether, and it marked me…

Try this same practice now with another object that you find grotesque or repulsive. This could be a dirty dish, a dead bug, or a picture of a political figure who irks you. Set a timer for ten minutes, fix your gaze on this new teacher, let your inner narrator speak and your eyes play tricks, then wait. Wait for something new to arise. When you have completed the ten-minute practice, reflect on your experience:

I named the grotesque teacher…
My mind rattled with…
I wanted to look away, but I…
I wanted to see…
I did not want to see…
Suddenly, the teacher changed and became…
I noticed…
I wondered…
I realized…
In that moment, I became…
I see now that…
Shadow is…
Shadow is not…

Breathe. When you feel ready, underline your medicinal phrases. Divine a certain poetic elixir from your word-witchery, and use these words to complete the second prompt:

The ether marked me [how the ether marked you from the first
   prompt]
I marked the ether [your underlined words]

Ether Presence III: The Language We Do Not Yet Speak

"I summoned ghosts, played with pendulums, and arranged all my crystals just so. But, all the while, I found myself unsettled by a deeper desire to learn a language I did not yet speak. I set the fire not out of malice but out of a need to move beyond the beauteous tools, these things I know so well, and into the dark unknown."

Our language is slow to evolve. As our dualistic thinking begins to crumble, we will require new words and new myths that transcend both linear time and binary understanding. Our language is linear; we read in straight lines, with clear beginnings and punctuated, finite endings. Our language also reinforces opposition. We may hear the word *start*, but our understanding is "not the end." What we need is a thousand words for the in-between.

Our academic training fools us into thinking we will not succeed in this life if we do not sculpt our language to suit the elite's version of eloquent. We slowly learn to not break the rules, to not dare to deviate, all the while understanding that nothing and everything is capitalized, words are rarely sufficient for describing deep emotional experiences, and the truest ending of most sentences is an ellipsis and not a period.

A Witch understands the power of naming and the power of silence. It takes a long time to arrive at the right names for our memories and our dream visions, if we ever do dare to speak such labels. It takes time to sculpt the poetry of a life. In this moment, consider what you might call the next chapter of your life, if it is beginning on the next new moon. List as many adjectives and strange descriptors as you can for your state of being; then knit them together with hyphens, peculiar symbols, and creative misspellings.

I met the poetry of my life, and it marked me...

Continue this process now. Let it be liberatory. If the word cannot be found, draw a spiral, a star, or another symbol that gets closer to your meaning than any single word can. Create your own language now, and tell of your vision for this next chapter in your story.

It began on an ordinary not-evening when...
In the sky that was my ground, I saw...
In the clouds that were the mirror, I witnessed...
I danced the dance of dreams and became...
I was there, I was not there, and...
You won't know this word, but I do, and it is...
When I say "fate," I really mean...
When I say "Witch," I really mean...
There was no ending to this time of...
I am...
I am...
I am...

When you are ready, return to what you have written and read it aloud. Underline the words and phrases that feel untraditional; then use these to complete the second prompt:

> *The poetry of my life marked me* [how the poetry of your life marked you from the first prompt]
> *I marked the poetry of my life* [your underlined words]

Ether Presence IV: To Be a Witch

> *"To be a Witch is more than the practice of the Craft....*
> *It is an embrace of the name Witch, a claiming it for one's own,*
> *and a commitment to a beginning rather than an end.*
> *The Witch is no master but an eternal student."*

To be in conversation is to be an eternal student. There can be no permanent mastery when life is change, and our spiritual journey, whether or not we have claimed the name Witch, is and has always been cyclical. There is no permanent plateau of understanding to be reached, no irrevocable wisdom-keeper title granting us permission to stop listening, growing, and transforming. To be a Witch is to be in metamorphosis and to find an exquisite comfort there in the cocoon.

What name do you feel ready to claim now, at this point in your journey? Perhaps it is *Witch*, or perhaps it is something else, something unique to you. Ask yourself: *Who am I?* Then ask: *Who am I really?* Listen to the silence until the name arrives.

> *I found my new name, and it marked me...*

Consider now all the implications of this extraordinary name. What memories does it evoke? What emotions does it ignite? What stories, deities, or other knowings do you associate with this name? Tell the tale of this new name now, letting a secret or two spill onto the page.

> *This is the tale of my new name, and my new name is...*
> *Had I heard this name ten years ago, I might have wondered...*
> *It's a name an elder version of me can be proud of, I think, because...*

If this new name is a tapestry, it's full of vibrant colors like...
If this name has a shadow side, it's called...
If I befriend this monster, my new name becomes...
I am the Witch of...
My new name makes me ready for a new...
Watch me become...

Read back through the writing and see if you can find a short incantation for your new name, a phrase you might begin to recite each day as a small ceremony of claiming this version of you, of growing into the name you have been given by the ether, by the wild unseen. Underline this incantation and use it to complete the second prompt:

My new name marked me [how your new name marked you
    from the first prompt]
I marked my new name [your underlined incantation]

❦ Ether Spell: Naming the Patterns ❦

This is a simple act of seer's discernment. Whatever month you find yourself in, begin one year ago, and make a list of the months by name. You will have thirteen total. If you are reading this in October, begin with October of the previous year and list each month until this October. The month you are in now will then be listed twice.

Once you have your list of months, consider what you would name as the main theme for each month. Approach this somewhat playfully. You cannot possibly distill your entire monthlong experience into a single theme, so allow your memory to be oracle and simply go with the first theme that seems to resurface. You might revisit your old calendars to jog your memory. Begin with the first month from one year ago and name a theme for each month in three words or less.

Look now at the story being told. Do you see any patterns or visible trends in these themes? Given where you have been, can you predict where you might be going?

You can apply this same tool to the previous three- or even nine-year cycle, but when working with longer durations, you might find that naming seasons is better than single months. There will, of course, be long periods of time in shadow if you are working with several years of experience. Name what you can and leave the rest out.

What story are you living out loud now? Can you see a clear beginning, rise, climax, fall, and resolution in any of your themes? Can you discern whether you are just beginning a new story now, reaching the pivotal moment, or starting to find resolution?

Pair this work with your more oracular knowledge, with the omens you are receiving from dreams and nature, with the other insights you are gathering from the ether. Let it be another lens to look through. And so it is.

Ether Visions

What do you see when you close your eyes? You might say *nothing*, but even nothing is something. Even that warm glow behind your lids or the strange lines left by the light are *something*. We are so quick to rush to the answer, are we not? In school, we learned to always seek an answer, to see every question mark as a prod.

If we are arriving at a new language for these new times, we must learn to allow questions to remain questions. Not every mystery wants solving. Not every shadow wants the light.

Ether Vision I: A Subtle Wink

"The Mystery winks at us time and time again,
offering us the evidence we seek with an open but unaggressive
hand. Our training has taught us to not believe in something,
despite all our sensory input proving its truth, unless it
thunders into the room and grabs our face in both hands."

We require certain conditions in order to see the subtle energies that always surround us. Some of us require stillness and silence. Others also require a certain amount of time spared for a disciplined practice of simply being. All of us require safety. Our biology keeps our senses attuned to what might most threaten our bodies; since subtle energies are rarely an imminent threat, our eyes will see the moving car before they see a ghost. We will hear humans talking before we hear the ancestors singing. This does not mean we need to remove ourselves from the built and busy world in order to connect with the unseen realm, but it does mean we need to tend to our nervous systems wherever we are, should we desire to hear the ethereal language.

Consider a moment, a memory, when you felt you received a message from the wild unseen. Maybe one of your beloved dead dropped a feather in your path, or you dreamed of a loving spirit you remember from childhood. Describe this memory now, to begin this entry in your Book of Ether:

I found the wild unseen, and it marked me…

An important guideline when working with the spirit realm is this: just because you *can*, does not mean you must. You do not have a responsibility to be a practicing medium simply because you have a gift for talking to the dead. We all have times in our lives when the subtle realm is not our greatest concern. Ask yourself to what extent you would like the ethereal to support you. How do you wish to be held by your ancestral lines, the loving dead, your future kin, the elementals, and even your dreams? You are, of course, already held and supported by all these seemingly invisible forces, but name your ideal vision for how you might commune with what most folks do not readily see. This practice is part intention setting, part manifestation writing.

I wake from dreams that show me…
I listen to the sounds of birdsong and hear…
I am met by my grandmother's ghost when…
The greatest oracle is my…
In the dark, I can see…
In the light, I can see…
The full moon shows me exactly how…
The new moon offers me an invitation toward…
I am a Witch of the wild unseen, and I am in conversation with…

Pay attention to any small sensations in your body now. Breathe from the belly and hum. Rock gently from side to side. Stay with this for a full three minutes if you are able; this is a simple practice for calming the nervous system, for attuning to the present moment. When you are ready, return to your writing and underline the words and phrases that feel right and true in your body; use these to finish the second prompt:

The wild unseen marked me [how the wild unseen marked you
   from the first prompt]
I marked the wild unseen [your underlined words]

Ether Vision II: The Ancestral Story

"We are the medicine."

To commune with the ethereal means to acknowledge the ancestral conversation, to hold the long-vision, and to realize we are but a single breath in the one long ancestral life. There are parts of your life, parts you may take for granted, that your great-great-grandmothers prayed for. This is absolutely not to say you should feel endlessly grateful no matter the landscape of your life or be fiercely optimistic in the face of so many atrocities occurring within the collective, but rather to say you are, in part, the very medicine your lineages required. Who are you in your grand ancestral story? Are you the mage? The innocent? The warrior? What soul-destined role do you feel you are playing in this one lone chapter of the epic bible that is your family's story?

I found the ancestral story, and it marked me…

Consider the primary Jungian archetypes now. To what extent do you embody each of these mythic characters?

I see magick in all things. I am the mage, and I am transforming…
I see patterns everywhere. I am the crone-sage, and I am study-
   ing…
I am in training. I am the warrior, and I am fighting for…
I am sovereign. I am the ruler, and I guide my people toward…
I am in love with the ordinary. I am the realist, and I have named
   the mundane…
I see beauty in this wild world of ours. I am the lover, and I am in
   a relationship with…
I welcome any invitation from the heart. I am the seeker, and I
   am looking for…
I can laugh in the face of chaos. I am the joker, and I see humor
   even in…

I speak the language of infinite possibilities. I am the visionary, and I invite…

I see the necessity of destruction. I am the rebel, and I am shedding…

I give and receive in balance. I am the caregiver, and I nurture…

I weave the old to create the new. I am the maker, and I am sculpting…

Consider which of the twelve prompts most intrigued you. Underline the words and phrases you wrote that feel potent; then use these to complete the second prompt:

The ancestral story marked me [how the ancestral story marked you from the first prompt]

I marked the ancestral story [your underlined words]

Ether Vision III: Washing the Dust

"On this night and every night, I am stripping away the day's layers of beliefs that are not mine, vows I did not take, and any accumulated dust from others' sympathies or disdain."

A Witch understands that discernment is integral to effective spell casting. We wish to welcome only what is truly ours, what we really desire rather than what we have been told by others we should desire. Immersed in a culture that is constantly trying to trick us away from the lives we know we want, we have a vital need to take regular inventories, to reflect on how far we have come and where we still would like to go.

Consider how many beliefs you have shed over the years, how many new names you have claimed, and how many lands have held you. Consider all you have composted in order to cultivate new ground, and consider what you still might like to plant here in this fertile soil. Describe these considerations now and begin this entry in your Book of Ether:

I found this new ground, and it marked me…

Wash the dust now. Reflect on what you have released and what you have called in just within the past year.

Last year at this exact time, I was washing the dust of…
I was calling in…
As the moons waxed and waned, I let go of the name that…
I welcomed a new, radical way of being and called it…
When the days grew warmer, I shed the skin of…
When the nights grew longer, I lit candles for…
Now, beneath this wild and holy sun, I am planting the seeds of…
I am washing the dust of…

Look to your patterns now. Invite the archetype of the crone-sage to step into your body and help you see a clear and visible cycle you continue to live so much it might feel like home. Do not name this particular pattern as good or bad. Let it be. When you feel ready, return to the writing and underline the sharp words and phrases, the language that feels particularly poetic, and complete the second prompt:

This new ground marked me [how the new ground marked you
    from the first prompt]
I marked this new ground [your underlined words]

Ether Vision IV: The Spirit Wakes Wild

"Blessed be this mist-filled morning, for the spirit wakes wild.
I am choosing to hand-brew this day out of sweet gratitude and pure
joy, spiced to perfection and served still steaming. I am welcoming
what comes and staying steadfast in my sovereignty. I am
a child of the earth and water, well versed in the languages of fire
and air, and I am at home in all the spaces between."

There are parts of our lives where we are naturally tame, where we conform to laws and social conventions, but our spirits and our souls are always wild. The spirit, that integral part of our psyches that connects us to the enduring sacred, and the soul, that unique aspect of ourselves that renders us *not* separate but certainly extraordinary, are older than these powers that be. Our souls are older than ancient. Our spirits are wiser than genius, and every day we rise from our beds as innocents.

I saw my innocent spirit, and it marked me…

Write a morning incantation now, a prayer to be spoken when you wake that reminds you to stay curious, to look to the trees as teacher, to seek input from the dirt more than from the glowing screen.

On this, the day of all days, may I remember to…
I will find great wisdom in the face of…
May I hum a soft song called…
To the wilds, I say…
To my own soul, I vow…
To my spirit that always wakes wild, I howl…

Read your morning prayer aloud and notice when your voice grows loud. When do your words ignite an inner fire? Underline these words, and use them to complete the second and final prompt:

My innocent spirit marked me [how your spirit marked you from the first prompt]
I marked my innocent spirit [your underlined words]

❧ *Ether Spell: Asking the Dream-Weaver* ❧

Our dreams are always trying to heal us. We are creatures born with a built-in divination system, but we are no longer taught to speak the language of dreams, our most personal oracle. The most important first step in dream work is to begin tracking your dreams. We all dream, though we may not remember what we dream.

When you begin marking what memories you have of your dreams — though they may seem small, fragmented, or unimportant — you are showing the dream-weaver, that wild hag who weaves away in your psychic house, that you are paying attention. You may find that your dreams become more fruitful the more you track them, and you will begin to discern the unique language your dreams speak only to you. You are rich in this language. You are wealthy in dream symbols and story.

Before you go to sleep, ask your dream-weaver for a telling dream. Be as specific as you can. Envision what your dream-weaver looks like and imagine yourself giving them a symbol of what you would like a dream to focus on. Try to speak to the dream-weaver in the same language you find in your dreams. For instance, if you know a red rose represents love to you and you would like a dream to grant you clarity on a particular relationship, give the dream-weaver a rose in this initial meeting. Set the intention to remember the dream messages you receive.

When you wake, if you received a telling dream, write down as much as you remember. Ask yourself to name the symbols. What objects did you dream of, and what might those objects represent outside the context of the dream? What was the nature of the dreamscape? Were you in a calm pasture or amid an apocalyptic wildfire? If so, what does this environment represent? What were the actions you were taking? Were you running, dancing, making love? What do these actions mean to you? Get underneath the objective description and personalize every single potential symbol. Make note of all these symbols and re-create the dream description by stitching these notes together.

Not every dream is a prophecy, but you might look for what events occur within three days. Keep track of your dreams that do seem to hold some oracular knowledge, and notice what distinguishes these dreams from the others. All patterns are relevant in dream work. Discount nothing. Think of the process like learning a shared language between you and the dream-weaver, between who you are on the surface and who you are inside the ancient well of your subconscious.

Those who speak the language of dreams cannot possibly dismiss the power of the unseen, the depth of the collective unconscious that unites us all, the reason why myths across all cultures contain shared symbology. Our dreams show us our uniqueness and individuality, yes, but also how intimately connected to the beyond-humanity community, to the creaturely realm and wild unseen, we have always been. And so it is.

Testament to Ether

The fifth and final Heathen Testament will be your Testament to Ether. Begin by writing an invocation to the ether element. You may use the prompts I offer here or create your own:

This is my testament of cosmic dust, moonlight, and dark matter.
I am the sound of a sun being born, and I am…

I am asking unanswerable questions of…
To the ether, I say…

Go back through your Ether Reflections, Presences, and Visions, and look to the last line from all twelve journal entries. Stitch these together to become your "Ether Verses":

Verse 1: I marked the void…
Verse 2: I marked the sacred…
Verse 3: I marked death…
Verse 4: I marked the Witch wound…
Verse 5: I marked the edge…
Verse 6: I marked the ether…
Verse 7: I marked the poetry of my life…
Verse 8: I marked my new name…
Verse 9: I marked the wild unseen…
Verse 10: I marked the ancestral story…
Verse 11: I marked this new ground…
Verse 12: I marked my innocent spirit…

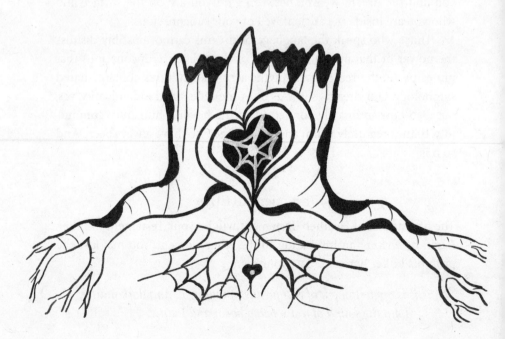

Complete the final prompt below. Then read your testament aloud in a sacred place, and if possible, follow the reading with a time of silence. Be witnessed and mirrored by those loving ghosts who know you best. And so it is.

I am here, held by the ether, and I know…

Possible Additions to Your Book of Ether

- Create a "wild divination" recipe, a toolkit for oracle work where each object is ethically sourced from nature. Go on an intentional wander and gather thirteen objects that are not too fragile. Kill nothing. Let all be found. Leave a gift to the land in return for every rock, twig, and bone. Write your own correspondences once you have collected your pieces. What does each object mean to you? If you allow each object to be teacher, what lessons does it have? Maybe a black river stone represents shadow, or a rose thorn represents boundaries. You decide. Place each object in a bag or basket. Reveal what each object means in your journal; then practice working with your kit by asking a question and pouring the objects from your bag or basket. What do you see in the odd constellation that is here?
- Design your ideal death ritual. Write your eulogy. Whom do you wish to speak? What stories do you want shared? What songs do you want sung? Where and how do you wish to be laid to rest?
- Rewrite your favorite fairy tale containing the hag archetype. Let her become heroine instead of villain and maybe, just maybe, cast yourself as her. What about your own story is revealed when you become the hag?

Holy Wild Spell: Gifting the Grimoire

Now that your grimoire has been written, consider gifting this book. You might tuck it away and give it to yourself nine days, nine months, or nine years in the future. You might hold on to it until the time comes for your child to receive it or leave it beside an elder's bed. Consider the wealth of memories woven into this book you have written, a book that could not have been written at any other time by any other hand. Consider the reflections and the visions, the musings and the images. What timely beauty your grimoire holds! What poetry and spirit are housed in those pages. And so it is.

CONCLUSION

*T*hese are tenderizing times. We are creatures being slowly but surely softened by uncertainty, as our rigid visions of a gleaming modern future are eroded by the floodwaters, by the wildfires, by the storms of reckoning. If we chose to be here for this moment, what purpose might our poetry, our Witchcraft, our voice, and our art serve?

The remedy for apathy is awe. We will not reason our way to redemption. We are holding the tension of the times in our bodies, and the most vital medicine we have is to become a living altar to grief and gratitude, to do what ancestral healing we can, to weep at the beauty of the wild dawn and build small temples from broken fence posts and stone.

We must be wary of over-romanticizing this apocalypse, yes, but neither can we be stunned into fear by the coming shifts. We must grant ourselves and one another immense care, the same care we might offer to a frightened child. *I hear you, and I see you. You are loved.*

We are travelers lost in a wilderness, holding outdated maps. No one will do this well. None of our old, reactive measures will make sense. Our best policies may fail, in part because we have not arrived at the language we need. Laws are not sculpted or painted, after all. We organize around shared meaning, but what if that shared meaning is, for now, some unnameable thing we can only dance around, never grasping and only glimpsing? What if we, quite literally, have no words for this?

As our communicative forms shift, as our words become ash in the wind, it will be our dualities that die first, having no voice to shelter them any longer. Our comfort can then come only from being fiercely present to the moment. Our solace no longer exists out there, somewhere in the distant yet-to-come, some brightly lit heaven awaiting us after the here and now becomes a corpse. That thing called *hope* has always sent us away from the present moment, luring us into the linear, keeping our eyes fixed forward. Hope is not a solution, but neither is sorrow.

The Witch lives on the fringes so that they can better see the whole. Standing at the center, you can see only so much. From those forbidden outskirts, you can see possibilities the center has never even dreamed of. What do you see now if you hold the tension between possibility and impossibility, between the hope for a conscious beyond-human community and the sorrow over the myths of modernity that have failed to fruit? If you breathe and break the cage of linear time around every cell in your body, hold the potential for both immense evolution and irrevocable extinction in your guts, and let a sound climb your spine, what song do you start singing?

This is the song of the moment, the lyricless hymn of the Holy Wild. Can you hear it? It is the universal, enduring, numinous sound of all. The Irish call it the *oran mór*, the great song. There is an infinite nature to this sound, a subtle but ubiquitous defiance of hard boundaries in both space and time. It is primarily a song of belonging, the resonance that unites us all in a shared awe.

The medicine for these times is kinship with what is and has always been, the elements that are here on this planet, gifted us by dead stars. If you feel you are here for a reason, you are right. If you cannot articulate the hows or the whys, stop trying. Stay malleable. Befriend adaptation. Imagine new futures and invite your ancestors who have seen such things before — who stood singing on the cliffside while the world they knew ended — to imagine with you. The story is larger and longer than us, larger and longer than what could ever appear on a screen. We are a single thread in the vast rainbow tapestry of time.

We are orphans of modernity, yes, but we are also makers, dreamers, and Witches capable of miracle-level creativity. This is not a call to end resistance by any means. This is a call to go beyond the available possibilities. This is a call to not just question everything but to let those questions go unanswered and find an odd and unnameable power in the confusion. This is a call to carry the older-than-ancient wisdom forward, heal what wounds from recent centuries we can, and sense the ephemeral seduction in the present.

This is the call of the Holy Wild, and you are here because your soul has already answered. Here we are, marked by awe and wonder. Here you are, making the world.

ACKNOWLEDGMENTS

To the hairy potter I call husband, thank you for cooking for me, our children, and the circle of Witches who come to visit us on the haunted land you tend so well. To Bodhi and Sage, thank you for choosing me as your mother and for choosing to be born in these times. To those whom I have been blessed to call teacher — including Bayo Akomolafe, Seán de Cantúail, and Dr. Clarissa Pinkola Estés — thank you for your immense wisdom, your writings, and your sacred work in the world. To the team at New World Library, including my editor Georgia Hughes, and to my agent Sheree Bykofsky, the deepest bows and wildest howls to you for all you have done and continue to do. To my beloved grandmother Grace, I miss you. Thank you for growing me up from my roots. To the snowy Mohawk land that has claimed me, I say thank you and vow to protect and tend you well.

NOTES

Love Letters on a Deathbed: An Introduction

p. 3   *"it's a good thing to hang on to the myth"*: Joseph Campbell, *Pathways to Bliss* (Novato, CA: New World Library, 2004), xxv.

p. 4   *If the etymology of* apocalypse: Michael Meade, *The Genius Myth* (Seattle: GreenFire Press, 2016), 21.

p. 8   *this rage is born of a threat:* See David Whyte, *Consolations* (Langley, WA: Many Rivers Press, 2015), 13–14.

Book One: The Book of Earth

p. 16   *Story Lantern: The Homecoming of Deer-Woman:* This tale is based on and inspired by the story of Sadhbh, the shape-shifting deer-woman in Irish mythology.

p. 23   *"There is a part of you, my love"*: Danielle Dulsky, *The Holy Wild* (Novato, CA: New World Library, 2018), 13–14.

p. 24   *"In our personal epic stories of wounding"*: Dulsky, *Holy Wild*, 14.

p. 26   *"This is me, and I have survived"*: Dulsky, *Holy Wild*, 17.

p. 26   *The stages of an initiation are the severance:* See Robert Moore, *The Archetype of Initiation* (Bloomington, IN: Xlibris, 2001).

p. 28   *"Every time the gritty marrow of the fruit"*: Dulsky, *Holy Wild*, 20.

p. 31   *"Rebellion against what is not ours"*: Dulsky, *Holy Wild*, 24.

p. 31   *In Jungian psychology, the archetype of the rebel:* See Carol Pearson, *What Stories Are You Living?* (Gainesville, FL: Center for Applications of Psychological Type, 2021).

p. 31   *white-body supremacy, and other like poisons:* See Resmaa Menakem, *My Grandmother's Hands* (Las Vegas: Central Recovery Press, 2017), for more information on white-body supremacy.

p. 33   *"May you be willing to exist on the fringes"*: Dulsky, *Holy Wild*, 33.

p. 34   *"Here, in ritual, we set boundaries"*: Dulsky, *Holy Wild*, 34.

p. 36   *"Recall the wisdom of your grandmothers"*: Dulsky, *Holy Wild*, 39.

p. 39   *"The descent is necessary"*: Dulsky, *Holy Wild*, 41.

p. 40   *"We tell ourselves we cannot have what we truly desire"*: Dulsky, *Holy Wild*, 42–43.

p. 41   *The Irish Goddess of sovereignty, Queen Maeve:* See Sylvia Brinton Perera, *Celtic Queen Maeve and Addiction* (North Beach, ME: Nicolas Hayes, 2001), for more information on Maeve's mythology.

p. 42   *"Now, bewitch this garden-hell"*: Dulsky, *Holy Wild*, 57.

p. 43   *"She saw herself handcrafting a new life"*: Dulsky, *Holy Wild*, 59–60.

Book Two: The Book of Water

p. 50   *Story Lantern: The Queen of Holy Intoxication:* This tale is based on and inspired by the story of Maeve in Irish mythology.

p. 61   *"If Earth is the place from which we rise"*: Dulsky, *Holy Wild*, 61.

p. 62   *"Just for today, let's be Priestesses"*: Dulsky, *Holy Wild*, 73–74.

p. 63   *"I am undone"*: Dulsky, *Holy Wild*, 79.

p. 64   *"The new moon is a cyclical vow"*: Dulsky, *Holy Wild*, 81.

p. 65   *A threshold crossing done with intention:* See Bill Plotkin, *Journey into Soul Initiation* (Novato, CA: New World Library, 2021), 109–11, for more information on threshold-crossing rituals.

p. 67   *"We must have joy in our Craft"*: Dulsky, *Holy Wild*, 82.

p. 68   *"I am softening my gaze"*: Dulsky, *Holy Wild*, 88.

p. 69   *"This is my benediction, my body prayer"*: Dulsky, *Holy Wild*, 100.

p. 70   *"Every spell she casts is an affirmation"*: Dulsky, *Holy Wild*, 102.

p. 73   *"The fertile dark all artists draw from"*: Dulsky, *Holy Wild*, 107.

p. 74   *"Come inside, and permit me to pour"*: Dulsky, *Holy Wild*, 108.

p. 75   *what the Irish might call eternal time:* See John O'Donohue, *Anam Cara* (New York: HarperCollins, 1997), 176–78.

p. 76   *"This eerie night belongs to me"*: Dulsky, *Holy Wild*, 110.

p. 76 *"A stretch of sea coast with no people"*: Martin Prechtel, *The Smell of Rain on Dust* (Berkeley, CA: North Atlantic Books, 2015), 47.

p. 77 *"Water will cleanse away what no longer belongs"*: Dulsky, *Holy Wild*, 110.

Book Three: The Book of Fire

p. 86 *Story Lantern: The Ire of the Fallen Mother*: This story is based on and inspired by the story of Macha from Irish mythology.

p. 92 *"For our ancestors, fire was the center point"*: Dulsky, *Holy Wild*, 115.

p. 93 *"You must reclaim the flames"*: Dulsky, *Holy Wild*, 117.

p. 94 *"Only when seen from the ground of destiny"*: Michael Meade, *Fate and Destiny* (Seattle: GreenFire Press, 2012), 5.

p. 95 *"Waste no more time here"*: Dulsky, *Holy Wild*, 122.

p. 97 *"With this blood, I thee wed"*: Dulsky, *Holy Wild*, 128.

p. 101 *"It is not a daily investment of strong will"*: Dulsky, *Holy Wild*, 133.

p. 102 *"There is a rage that limits us"*: Dulsky, *Holy Wild*, 138.

p. 103 *"Fire is the original oracle"*: Dulsky, *Holy Wild*, 141.

p. 105 *"You are not your wounds"*: Dulsky, *Holy Wild*, 143.

p. 108 *"The fire element is not only a symbol"*: Dulsky, *Holy Wild*, 144.

p. 109 *"Consider times in your life, my love"*: Dulsky, *Holy Wild*, 149–50.

p. 110 *"Do not succumb to apathy"*: Dulsky, *Holy Wild*, 152.

p. 112 *"Listen, lover"*: Dulsky, *Holy Wild*, 156–57.

p. 114 *do not go quietly into that good night*: Dylan Thomas, "Do not go gentle into that good night," *The Poems of Dylan Thomas* (New York: New Directions Publishing Corporation, 2003), 239.

Book Four: The Book of Air

p. 120 *Word-Spell: Songs of Breath and the Wild Hunt*: "The Wild Hunt," originally published on *The House of Twigs*, https://thehouseoftwigs.com/2019/09/21/the-wild-hunt-a-drum-and-bone-omen-of-underworld-ceremony.

p. 122 *Story Lantern: The Blood Cloak*: This story is inspired by and based on the tales of Brighid from Irish mythology.

p. 127 *"The Witch of Sacred Love is an openhearted lover"*: Dulsky, *Holy Wild*, 161–62.

p. 128 *"The healer's road is long and unpaved"*: Dulsky, *Holy Wild*, 169.

p. 130 *"Hail and welcome, she who is feared"*: Dulsky, *Holy Wild*, 170–71.

p. 131 *"One day, I may come to know a wise Wolf-Woman"*: Dulsky, *Holy Wild*, 173.

p. 134 *"Ours is a land of soulful diversity"*: Dulsky, *Holy Wild*, 188.

p. 136 *"In our collective evolution"*: Dulsky, *Holy Wild*, 189.

p. 136 *Perhaps our human community*: See Bill Plotkin, *Nature and the Human Soul* (Novato, CA: New World Library, 2008).

p. 137 *"This is what binds the circle together"*: Dulsky, *Holy Wild*, 193.

p. 138 *"Oh, dearest innocent"*: Dulsky, *Holy Wild*, 194–95.

p. 141 *"The magick of the air element"*: Dulsky, *Holy Wild*, 196.

p. 143 *"I am the Witch of Sacred Love"*: Dulsky, *Holy Wild*, 201–2.

p. 144 *"In moving from air to ether"*: Dulsky, *Holy Wild*, 204.

p. 145 *"In lieu of flowers, please send"*: Dulsky, *Holy Wild*, 204.

Book Five: The Book of Ether

p. 153 *Story Lantern: Return of the Mist Dwellers*: This story is inspired by the Goddess Danu and the Tuatha Dé Danann from Irish mythology.

p. 155 *"Ether is the space between"*: Dulsky, *Holy Wild*, 207.

p. 157 *"We face our most significant human challenge"*: Dulsky, *Holy Wild*, 209.

p. 159 *"Deeply embedded fears of the dark"*: Dulsky, *Holy Wild*, 210–11.

p. 160 *"No more do your threats of hellfire"*: Dulsky, *Holy Wild*, 216.

p. 163 *"The heathen, the Witch, and the wild woman"*: Dulsky, *Holy Wild*, 223.

p. 164 *The trickster archetype lives on the outskirts*: See Lewis Hyde, *Trickster Makes This World* (New York: Farrar, Straus and Giroux, 1998), for more information on the trickster archetype.

p. 165 *"I am both sovereign and at one with all that is"*: Dulsky, *Holy Wild*, 225.

p. 167 *"I summoned ghosts, played with pendulums"*: Dulsky, *Holy Wild*, 230.

p. 169 *"To be a Witch is more than the practice"*: Dulsky, *Holy Wild*, 233.

p. 171 *"The Mystery winks at us"*: Dulsky, *Holy Wild*, 237.

p. 173 *"We are the medicine"*: Dulsky, *Holy Wild*, 248.

p. 173 *Consider the primary Jungian archetypes now*: See Pearson, *What Stories*.

p. 174 *"On this night and every night"*: Dulsky, *Holy Wild*, 249.

p. 175 *"Blessed be this mist-filled morning"*: Dulsky, *Holy Wild*, 251.

p. 177 *re-create the dream description*: This practice is inspired by a lecture by Dr. Clarissa Pinkola Estés from her Singing Over the Bones training in August 2019.

Conclusion

p. 182 *The Irish call it the* oran mór: See Frank MacEowen, *The Mist-Filled Path* (Novato, CA: New World Library, 2002), 138–40.

ABOUT THE AUTHOR

*D*anielle Dulsky is a heathen visionary, Aquarian mischief maker, and word-witch. Danielle is the author of *The Sacred Hags Oracle* (New World Library, 2021), *Seasons of Moon and Flame* (New World Library, 2020), *The Holy Wild* (New World Library, 2018), and *Woman Most Wild* (New World Library, 2017) and the founder of the Hag School. She believes in the power of wild collectives and sudden circles of curious dreamers, cunning Witches, and rebellious artists, as well as the importance of ancestral healing, embodiment, and animism in fracturing the long-standing systems supporting white supremacy and environmental unconsciousness. Parent to two beloved wildlings and partner to a potter, Danielle fills her world with nature, family, and intentional awe.

DanielleDulsky.com
TheHagSchool.com